Electricity and

by Kim Fields

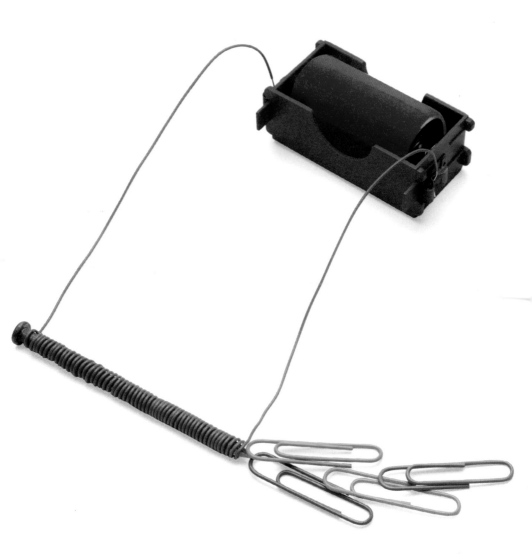

PEARSON
Scott
Foresman

DK

How does matter become charged?

Electric Charges

Touch a metal doorknob after running across a carpet. A spark of static electricity might give you a shock.

Atoms are the tiny building blocks of matter. Almost all atoms have three kinds of particles. Some particles have a negative charge. Some have a positive charge. Some particles have no charge. The number of negative and positive particles in matter is usually the same.

Sometimes an atom has more of one kind of particle than another kind. **Static electricity** is the result. *Static* means "not moving," and static electricity usually stays in one place. But eventually, it does move. It may move slowly or very quickly. Moving charges make electrical energy. This energy changes into heat, light, and sound energy.

Static Electricity

Storm clouds become charged when particles move between atoms. The positive particles usually gather near the top of the clouds. The negative particles move toward the bottom of the clouds. The static electricity is released as lightning. Lightning heats the air around it. The heated air glows. Lightning makes the sound that we call thunder.

How Charged Objects Behave

Objects with opposite charges are attracted to each other. An object with a positive charge and an object with a negative charge will pull toward each other. This attraction makes an electric force. An electric force is the push or pull between objects with opposite charges.

An object with a charge can attract something without a charge. Rub a blown-up balloon on your head. It picks up negative particles from your hair. This gives the balloon a negative charge. Then hold the balloon near lightweight objects that are neutral, such as small pieces of paper. The pieces of paper stick to the balloon! Eventually, the balloon loses its negative charge. The pieces of paper fall off.

An Electric Field

An electric field is the space around electrically charged objects. It is invisible. The electric field is strongest close to the charged object. It gets weaker as it gets farther away.

A negative electric field attracts positive charges. It pushes away, or repels, negative ones. A positive electric field attracts negative charges and pushes away positive ones.

These balloons have the same charge. They repel each other.

These balloons have opposite charges. They attract each other.

How do electric charges flow?

How Electric Charges Move

Most electricity moves. An electric charge in motion is called an **electric current.** An electric current travels quickly Electricity can be very dangerous. You cannot see it. Look at the circuit below. A circuit is a loop. Charges cannot flow through a circuit that has any breaks, or openings. The circuit must be closed. An open circuit has at least one break that stops the flow of charges.

A Closed Circuit

Energy source
Batteries cause the electric charges to flow.

Means of energy transfer
The charges flow through the wires.

Going with the Flow

An electric charge does not flow the same way through all materials. The atoms of some materials are charged more easily than others. These materials are called conductors. Most metals are good conductors. The copper wire in the circuit below is a good conductor. Silver is also a good conductor.

Electric charge moves through the atoms of some materials slowly. These materials are called insulators. Dry wood, rubber, plastic, and glass are good insulators. The wire in the picture is insulated. This stops the electric charges from traveling to other wires. The wire in each light bulb is made of a material with high resistance. **Resistance** means the material does not allow electric charges to flow easily.

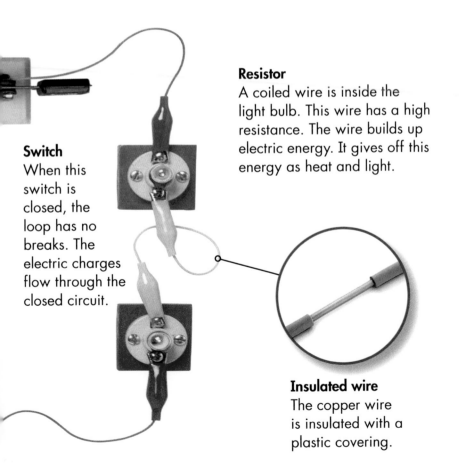

Resistor
A coiled wire is inside the light bulb. This wire has a high resistance. The wire builds up electric energy. It gives off this energy as heat and light.

Switch
When this switch is closed, the loop has no breaks. The electric charges flow through the closed circuit.

Insulated wire
The copper wire is insulated with a plastic covering.

Types of Circuits

In a **series circuit,** an electric charge can flow in only one path. Look at the string of lights. A power source is turned on. The charged particles in the wire flow in one direction around a loop. Each light bulb around the path receives the same amount of electrical energy. If all the bulbs are the same, each will have the same brightness.

If one bulb burns out, it opens the circuit. The electricity cannot cross the break in the circuit. The other bulbs won't receive the energy they need. So no bulbs are able to light.

In a series circuit, all items wired into the circuit share the electric current equally. Each item gets the same amount of current. Appliances need different amounts of current. Today series circuits are rarely used.

Series circuit

Parallel Circuits

A **parallel circuit** has two or more paths for electric charges to take. All the lights in a circuit don't go out when one light burns out. In a parallel circuit the main loop starts and stops at the power source. Along the loop there are smaller loops. Each smaller loop is a separate path for the electric charges. If electricity stops flowing through one of the smaller loops, it can still flow through the large loop.

Circuits used in buildings are parallel circuits. A parallel circuit can handle electric devices that need different amounts of current.

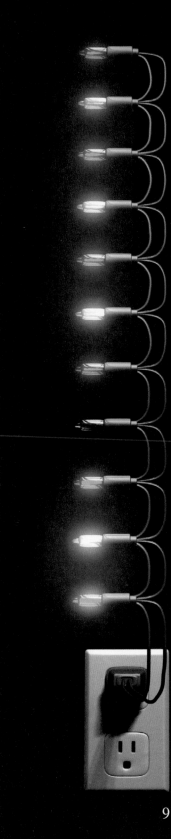

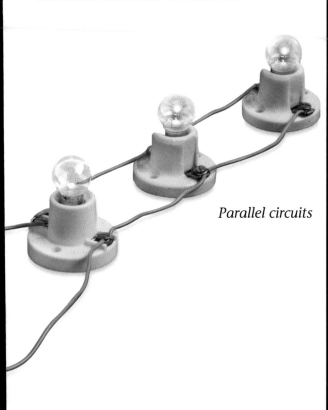

Parallel circuits

What are magnetic fields?

Magnetism

A magnet is an object that attracts other objects made of steel, iron, and certain other metals. **Magnetism** is the force that pushes or pulls magnetic items near a magnet.

Magnetic Fields

Magnets have an invisible field surrounding them. This is called a **magnetic field.** The shape of the magnetic field depends on the shape of the magnet. Look at the pattern of iron filings near the horseshoe magnet. The pattern is different from the pattern around the bar magnet on the next page. The magnetic fields have different shapes because the magnets have different shapes. Any magnetic field is strongest at the magnet's ends, or poles. The pushing or pulling force is also strongest at the poles.

Magnetic Poles

All magnets have a south-seeking pole and a north-seeking pole. Opposite poles have opposite charges. Opposite charges pull toward each other. Like charges push away from each other. The south-seeking pole on one magnet and the north-seeking pole on another magnet pull toward each other. But two south-seeking poles push apart.

Breaking a magnet into two parts makes two magnets. Each has a north-seeking pole and a south-seeking pole. The two poles of a magnet are like the two sides of a coin. You cannot have one without the other.

The Largest Magnet in the World

Ancient sailors used compasses. But they didn't know why the compasses worked. Then around 1600 a British scientist named William Gilbert claimed that the world's largest magnet is Earth! The huge magnetic field that surrounds Earth makes one end of a compass needle point north.

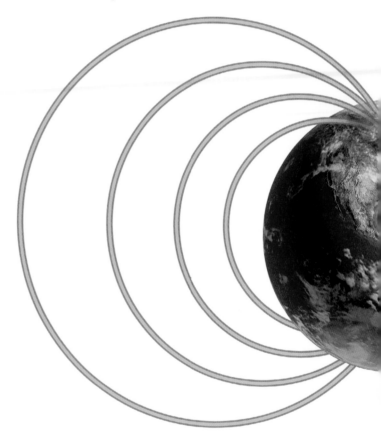

Earth's magnetic field is strongest at the poles. But Earth's magnetic poles are not the same as its geographic poles. The geographic poles are on Earth's axis. This is the invisible line that Earth rotates around. Earth's magnetic north pole is in Canada. It is about 1,000 kilometers (600 miles) from the geographic North Pole. The magnetic south pole is in the Southern Ocean near Antarctica.

Scientists don't know why Earth acts as a magnet. But they have an idea. Scientists think that Earth's outer core is made of iron. They think that this iron is so hot that it has melted. As Earth rotates, the liquid iron flows. The moving iron makes a magnetic field. The inner core is probably solid iron. It doesn't melt because it is under extremely high pressure.

Earth's axis

How Compasses Work

A compass is a small, handy tool. No matter where you are on Earth, one end of a compass needle will always point north. It is drawn to the pull of Earth's magnetic north pole. When you know which direction is north, you can easily find east, west, and south.

A compass needle has to be light. It must turn easily to work properly. The compass cannot be near a magnet. If it is, the needle will be pulled by the magnet. The needle will respond to the magnet's pull instead of Earth's pull.

The Northern Lights

The Aurora Borealis, or the Northern Lights, is a natural light show that is visible at different times during the year. Auroras come from charged particles given off by the Sun. These charged particles are pulled to Earth's magnetic north and south poles. The poles are the strongest parts of Earth's magnetic field. The particles crash into particles of gas in Earth's atmosphere. The crashes produce colorful light. Scientists have also seen auroras in Jupiter's atmosphere.

How is electricity transformed to magnetism?

Electromagnets

In 1820 scientist Hans Christian Oersted was showing how electric current flowed through a wire. He saw that the needle on a nearby compass moved each time he turned on the electric current. Oersted realized the flowing current made a magnetic field. This led to the invention of the electromagnet.

An **electromagnet** is a coil of wire wrapped around an iron core. An electromagnet changes electrical energy into magnetic energy. A current moving through the wire causes a magnetic field around the electromagnet. The wire loses its magnetic power when the current stops.

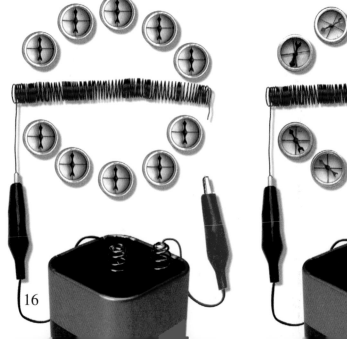
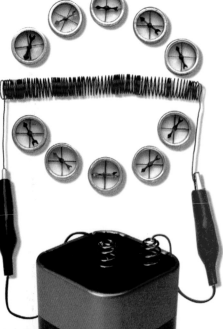

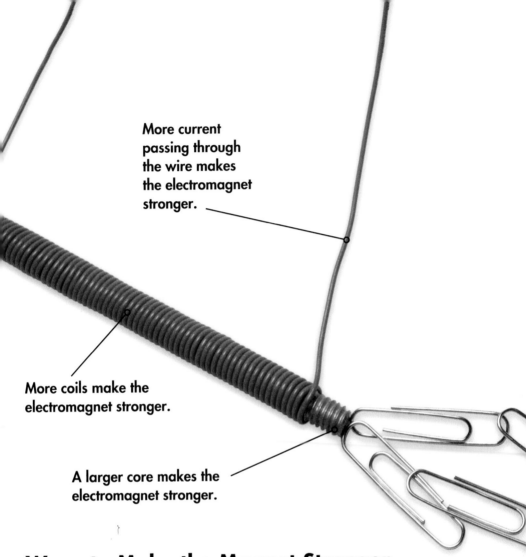

More current passing through the wire makes the electromagnet stronger.

More coils make the electromagnet stronger.

A larger core makes the electromagnet stronger.

Ways to Make the Magnet Stronger

An electromagnet has a south and north pole, just as a natural magnet has. You can change the strength of an electromagnet. To make an electromagnet stronger, you can increase the amount of current moving through the wire. You can add turns to the metal coil. A third way to make the electromagnet more powerful is to make the magnetic core larger.

Uses for Electromagnets

Electromagnets are used to lift heavy objects. Electromagnets are also in many machines that scientists and doctors use.

Electronic devices that you use each day have electromagnets. DVD players, fans, computers, and televisions work because of electromagnets. Electromagnets help change electric energy into magnetic energy and then into other kinds of energy.

How a Doorbell Works

Press the button on a doorbell. This closes the electrical circuit. The current flows to a part called the transformer. The transformer controls how much current is sent to the electromagnet. Electricity flowing into the coil of wire causes the electromagnet to become magnetized. This magnetism pulls up the contact arm. The arm is attached to the metal clapper. The clapper hits the bell. The bell rings. Magnetic energy has been changed into the sound you hear.

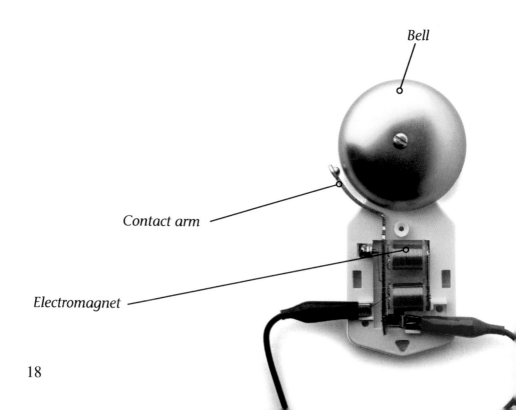

Bell

Contact arm

Electromagnet

Simple Electric Motor

Permanent magnet—works with the electromagnets in the armature. The north end of the permanent magnet pushes away the north end of the electromagnet. The south ends also push away from each other. This causes the axle to spin.

Armature or rotor—a set of electromagnets, each with thin copper wire coiled around it

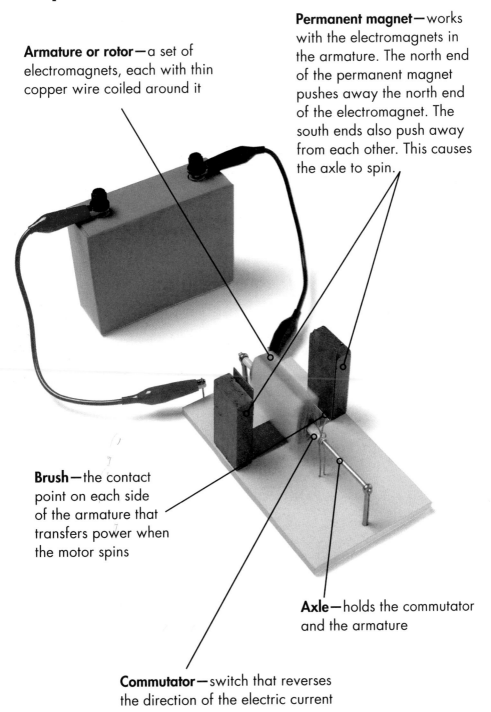

Brush—the contact point on each side of the armature that transfers power when the motor spins

Axle—holds the commutator and the armature

Commutator—switch that reverses the direction of the electric current

How is magnetism transformed to electricity?

Electrical Energy

Most people use electrical energy without thinking about it. They find it hard to think of life without electricity. The electrical energy that powers televisions, lamps, and refrigerators has come a long way.

We use magnetism to make electricity. We can make electricity by sliding coiled wire back and forth over a magnet. We can also make electricity by spinning the wire around a magnet.

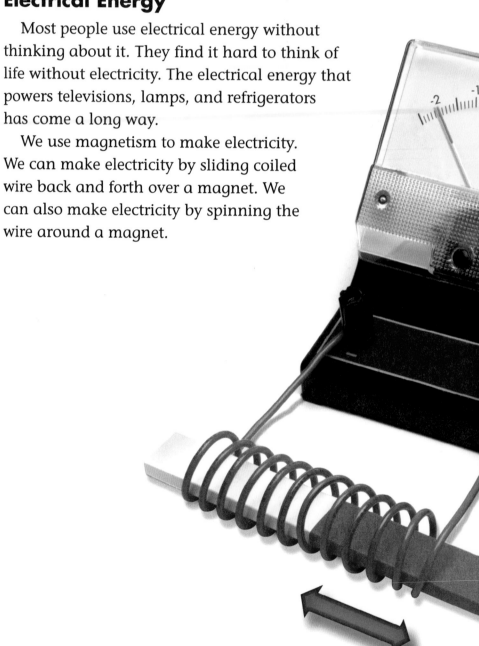

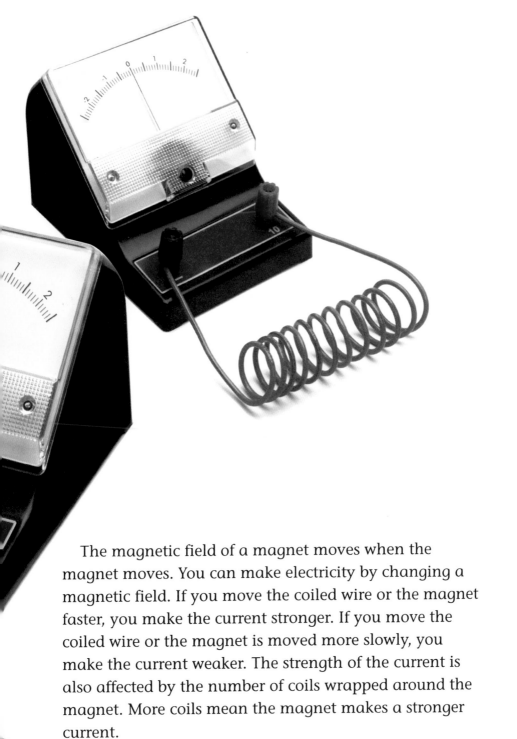

The magnetic field of a magnet moves when the magnet moves. You can make electricity by changing a magnetic field. If you move the coiled wire or the magnet faster, you make the current stronger. If you move the coiled wire or the magnet is moved more slowly, you make the current weaker. The strength of the current is also affected by the number of coils wrapped around the magnet. More coils mean the magnet makes a stronger current.

A Flashlight Without Batteries

Michael Faraday was a British scientist. In 1831 he invented a machine that used magnets to change motion into an electric current. He made electrical energy by turning a crank on the machine. He called this a dynamo. This is the same technology that 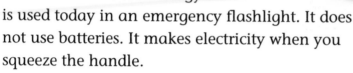 is used today in an emergency flashlight. It does not use batteries. It makes electricity when you squeeze the handle.

Currents Currently

A generator makes electric energy by turning coils of wire around powerful magnets. It uses magnets and wires to produce electrical energy. Most businesses, homes, and schools use electricity from generators.

Discoveries in Using Electrical Energy

Many people have made many discoveries about electricity. In the 1740s Benjamin Franklin and Ebenezer Kinnersley described electric charges as positive or negative. Zenobe Gramme developed the electric generator in 1870. Thomas Edison demonstrated the first light bulb in 1879. And those are just a few examples!

How Generators Are Powered

Some generators make electrical energy by using the energy of the wind. Others use falling water. Some generators are powered by steam. This steam may be from the hot temperatures deep below Earth's surface or from nuclear energy heating water. In each kind of generator, a coil of wire spins around a magnet. Electricity and magnetism work together in generators to provide energy for many things.

Glossary

electric current   an electric charge in motion

electromagnet   a core of iron with wire coiled around it; when electricity goes through the wire, it causes a magnetic field

magnetic field   an invisible field around a magnet where the force of magnetism can be felt

magnetism   a force that pushes or pulls magnetic materials near a magnet

parallel circuit   a circuit in which an electric charge can follow two or more paths

resistance   the ability of a substance to keep an electric charge from flowing through it easily

series circuit   a circuit in which electric charge flows in one path

static electricity   the result of positive and negative particles not in balance

MIRACLES
are Your Destiny!

EVANGELIST DEA WARFORD

Miracles Are Your Destiny!

Copyright 2021

Evangelist Dea Warford

Warford Ministries

www.deawarford.org

Edited by Linda Stephens

Cover and Formatting by

Shannon Herring

Published by

Pen & Power Publishing

Printed in the United State of America

978-1-7352994-4-0 Paperback

978-1-7352994-5-7 Hardback

Preface

(Pictured on the Front Cover is Dea, standing by a display case at the Heritage Center, Angelus Temple, Los Angeles, California. Shown are items left behind by disabled people, healed through the ministry of Aimee Semple McPherson. You will read more about this display case momentarily.)

"And God has placed in the church first of all apostles, second prophets, third teachers, then. . .*MIRACLES*."

If God "has placed in the church" miracles, then why are we not seeing more of them? You, like most Christians today, may have never even seen one in your entire life! Why is that? We explore that question in this book and unveil a remedy.

I am convinced that the greatest harvest of souls and a widespread, commonplace occurrence of amazing miracles are soon to happen in American churches and also in your own life! I wrote this book to inspire you and help prepare you for this last days move of God.

In the following pages, I share the story of my calling to work miracles and how I learned to do so.

Yes, I work miracles. But this book is just as much about you as it is about me. You, too, can and WILL work miracles. Let me prove it to you!

Are you ready to soon experience the most exciting adventures of your entire life? If you are, read on and . . .

EXPECT A MIRACLE!

Contents

Introduction

"The words of the Lord are great, Studied by all who have pleasure in them" (Psalm 111:2).

The first book I wrote, *EVANGELIST*, subtitled, *MY LIFE STORY: MY LIFE JOURNEY* (available for purchase at Amazon.com) is my autobiography wherein I describe my supernatural rescue from drowning as a four-year-old, my deliverance from a planned career in the Ku Klux Klan cult, my call to the ministry, the discovery of my life-partner, Kathy, and many other interesting experiences from my seven-decade (so far!) journey.

In *EVANGELIST,* I primarily focused on stories of the many souls I had won to Christ since I was 17 years old. In the last chapters, I gave helpful suggestions on how any Christian can personally lead souls to Christ. Have you personally led a soul to Christ lately? If not, you probably need to read my book!

When I first began writing *Evangelist*, I thought it would include the truths taught in this book, all contained in one volume. However, as I wrote, I soon realized that the first book's focus should be primarily on soul-winning and that I would need to write this additional volume. Two-hundred fifty or so pages were just not enough to complete my personal story and reveal the word God has given me for the church.

My controlling purpose for *Evangelist* was the following truth: Paul wrote in 2 Timothy 4:5, "do the work of an evangelist." He didn't say, "be an evangelist" (as I am sure relatively few are called to this full-time ministry!). Nevertheless, Paul wrote, in simple language:

"DO WHAT EVANGELISTS DO!"

I submit to you that every Christian should be doing what I, as an evangelist, strive to do, at least on a part-time basis.

So, what then does an evangelist do? I wrote extensively about that ministry in *Evangelist* from the perspective of decades of experiences of just one evangelist, me. Recounting many stories from my life and with the help of supporting scriptures, I sought to prove that the single most crucial work evangelists do is soul-winning (both one-on-one and corporately).

That is where this, my second book, comes into play. The title on this book's front cover, *Miracles are Your Destiny*, hints at what I spend many pages unveiling. Winning a soul to Christ is the greatest miracle anyone could experience. Yet, a soul-winning evangelist is called to do much more than preach and witness for Christ. He is described explicitly in Scriptures as a "Miracle Worker" (a truth I will establish in later chapters). There are many kinds of miracles, and miracles are not easy to achieve (that's why we call them miracles!).

In this volume, I will focus on three miracles:

- healing the sick

- casting out demons

- prophesying.

God has been training me to perform miracles for over five decades, so I strongly felt the need to share "my truths" with you. It may even be a minor miracle that you now have this book in your hands! I believe it will help birth in you the desire and the ability to work miracles!

Paul's suggestion (NO! It's a command!), "do the work of an evangelist," then means more than just soul-winning. It means every Christian should, as well as witnessing for Him, also expect and go after miracles!

If I were a betting man, I would bet that I have read more evangelists' biographies and probably have more of them in my office library than anyone reading this. Nothing fascinated me more in my younger years than reading about the miracles in the lives of American evangelists.

I had the privilege of attending the services of many famous evangelists, among them Oral Roberts, A.A. Allen, R.W. Shambach, and Kathryn Kuhlman. I marveled as I saw them moving in the miracle dimension and heard testimonies of healing or deliverance. I now understand that this fascination was the call on my life to do the same things they did!

"**Miracles**" are defined as "**welcome events that cannot be explained by natural or scientific laws and must be acts of supernatural agency.**"

There are many hurting, tormented, and hopeless souls whose lives can be changed only by the Hand of God, a supernatural agency. Would you like to be His Hand extended? Would you like to be a miracle worker? Would you like to personally see things happen on earth originating from the invisible realm? If so, God had YOU in mind when He led me to write this book.

Finish reading *MIRACLES ARE YOUR DESTINY*, and I predict, even dare prophesy:

You will soon see Miracles in your life!

PART ONE

HEALING THE SICK

"When I was two years old, I developed arthritis. It spread everywhere. My legs were becoming crippled. I had duck feet and couldn't run for half my life. I was on almost every medication there is for arthritis. Ever since I was a Christian, I was prayed for so many times. When I was ten, I ran for the first time. My joints started to become normal. They still hurt sometimes, but they weren't crippled anymore. I heard Dea was coming to town and read on the billboard to, "Expect a Miracle!" God said to come to this revival. Friday night, Dea prayed for me. I started to gag because there was a demon in me that was holding on to my arthritis. I felt that demon leave me. Ever since I have felt free. All weekend, I have not felt one pain or sore bone in my body since, except for growing pains. My left leg was shorter than my right because of the medicine I had taken when I was younger, but all day Saturday, I have had growing pains in my left leg, and they were the same size a day later. My jaw also had arthritis, and each side was different, but not anymore. Before, even when my joints weren't hurting, I could still feel my arthritis was there. Now, I can't feel anything. I could never wear dress shoes with big heels for more than an hour without pain. All Sunday morning, I wore my dress shoes, and not one hurt. Praise God, I know for sure that I am healed completely."

— JAMIE TUCKER
Butte, Montana

1

Aimee Semple McPherson

"How beautiful are the feet of those who preach the gospel of peace, Who bring glad tidings of good things!" (Romans 10:15).

I stared into the glass-encased collection of memorabilia from the life of the healing evangelist Aimee Semple McPherson (b. 1890, d. 1944). The displayed canes, crutches, and prosthetic devices had been left behind by those who had received a miracle through Aimee's prayers (see the front cover!).

That day a family friend brought me to see the famous Angelus Temple Church, which Aimee had built. The imposing three-story structure, constructed in 1923, seated 5,300 at the time and was just a few miles from downtown Los Angeles. We stood on the mezzanine for a few moments pondering about the people who once wore those wooden, metal, and leather devices. I was probably sixteen years old at the time. How could I have imagined that I was looking at my destiny!

LIFE Bible College was built by Aimee in 1926, right next door to the Temple. It was just a year or two later that I would be living at the LIFE dorms, also built as part of the campus of Angelus Temple. My first week of school in September 1966, I joined other first-year students enrolled in the Bible College on the same platform where Aimee had preached the gospel and healed the sick. We took turns sharing our stories of how God had brought us to the school. I gave my testimony of how God had saved me from a future career in the Ku Klux Klan (see my autobiographical book *EVANGELIST*). As I spoke that evening into that KFSG radio microphone, my voice would be broadcast into homes, a sound that would continue in all fifty states and foreign countries as I preached the gospel over the next half of a century.

Jack Hayford was present that evening. He was a professor at LIFE Bible College and only thirty-two years old. Later, he would become the founding pastor of the Church on the Way with thousands of members. He wrote over fifty books and hundreds of hymns and choruses. Jack was also, for a season, the President of the International Church of the Foursquare Gospel which Mrs. McPherson had also founded. Jack profoundly influenced my life, as I explained in my autobiography. During a freshman class in 1966 at LIFE, he told us:

> **"Aimee Semple McPherson was probably the outstanding woman in church history."**

Why would Jack say such a thing? What was his evidence? Let me share some of Aimee's accomplishments as my destiny is so intertwined with hers:

- She built Angelus Temple, the first mega-church in America, ministering to about 20,000 a week in that facility and often preached 22 times a week.

- The Foursquare Gospel Church Organization that she founded that same year would by 2020 comprise 90,000 churches and 8.8 million members in 146 countries.

- In 1926 LIFE Bible College was built next door to Angelus Temple. In 1990 the college moved to a new campus in San Dimas, California. The school is now called "LIFE Pacific University" (my daughter, Carissa, and son-in-law, Andy, are both professors there).

- Under Aimee's leadership, the Foursquare organization began a strong Christian camping program, with beautiful camps around the nation visited by thousands of children and youth. Camp Cedar Crest in the San Bernardino Mountains northeast of Los Angeles is where God saved me and called me to preach the gospel (which I share in my autobiography).

- She was one of the first to use radio to reach far and wide with the gospel, starting the KSFG radio station broadcasting from the Temple.

- Aimee was known for her dramatic illustrated sermons which were so professionally done that as many as 100 Hollywood actors would appear at one of her services.

- She published books, including her autobiography, *This is That.*

- Aimee wrote and staged original theatrical dramas and oratorios in Angelus Temple, wrote five operas and more than 200 songs and hymns.

Yet to me, by far, her greatest contribution to this planet was the miracle/healing ministry that God had given her. During a 1916 series of New York meetings, a woman with advanced rheumatoid arthritis was in Aimee's service. Aimee laid hands on her, and the woman was healed right before the congregation's eyes, her twisted neck suddenly straightened, and she was then able to walk out of the church, unassisted by her crutches.

Subsequently, this healing gift became a primary feature of her ministry, drawing curious crowds and sick and afflicted to her revivals. Blind eyes opened, deaf ears could hear, invalids brought by ambulances and laid on cots in the altar area were often able to walk away from the church, sending their ambulances home.

During the height of her ministry, it is estimated that four out of five people who came for healing, were. During this season, Aimee was on the first page of the Los Angeles Times newspaper on average three days a week.

Aimee preached what she coined "The Foursquare Gospel" which, to her, included the ministry of Jesus Christ as: (1) our Savior, (2) our Baptizer in the Holy Spirit, (3) our Great Physician, and (4) our Soon-Coming King (I would one day become an ordained Foursquare Gospel minister and preach those four aspects of the gospel).

It was the third emphasis, divine healing, that I discovered was a special call on my life. Over five decades after my first visit to Angelus Temple, I now realize that I carry within my soul the DNA of Aimee Semple McPherson. I am called to be an evangelist working miracles as she did. A Foursquare youth camp and a Foursquare Bible college became tools the Lord used to propel me towards my destiny.

Aimee was an early pioneer of the use of radio for evangelism. Decades after her death, her radio influence reached out to me (the "dead yet speaketh"—Hebrews 11:4 KJV)). I was seventeen years old and driving to Chaffey Community College to finish up some credits to graduate a year early from high school. I was planning on attending Cal Poly, Pomona to major in Social Science. My goal was to be Imperial Wizard of the Ku Klux Klan (my autobiography tells that story!).

As I switched between rock and roll stations on my car radio, I happened upon a fiery Evangelist, J. Charles Jessup. He preached loud, fast-paced, and compellingly. Inside I somehow felt that I needed to preach like that! I remember him describing how he held in his hands a jar with a cancerous tumor inside it which someone had passed after he prayed for them. My mind could visualize that cancer, and my spirit leaped at the thought of seeing such miracles.

August 1966, I went to Camp Cedar Crest with a cousin. There, I answered the first evening altar call to dedicate my life to Christ. A few mornings later, awakening about four AM, I felt the call to the ministry. I knelt at my bunk bed and, after mentioning a precondition (which I describe in my autobiography), I said, "I'll do my best to become a Foursquare Minister." Within weeks I was in Bible College and preparing to be just that.

While pastoring a church about a decade later, the Lord spoke to my heart, "You will always be a part of the Foursquare organization." So far, I heard right. This past year I received my Fifty-Year Gold Service Pin. Most of my ministry as an evangelist has been in Foursquare Churches, though I preach extensively also in our sister organization, the Assemblies of God, along with other denominations from time to time. I'd be tickled to preach in a Catholic Church, Kingdom Hall, or Mormon Temple if they'd let me!

My Call To Heal The Sick

On my second to the last night at Camp Cedar Crest in 1966, I was among other teenagers who were praying in the Prayer Room after the service. There was a girl there who couldn't talk. She wasn't mute, but she could just barely whisper for some unknown reason. We gathered around her and prayed for her healing. She wasn't healed that night. I was saddened and concerned about that. Pastor Austin Crager, who also happened to be my cabin counselor, was in the prayer room with us. I asked him, "What can we do for her?" He said, "Let's fast and pray tomorrow and we will pray for her again tomorrow night."

The next day, as a 17-year-old, was the first day I ever fasted. It wouldn't be the last. I had no idea at the time that fasting was a big part, historically speaking, of the life of an evangelist as he seeks God's power to heal the sick. I would read about that fact in many biographies of evangelists in my future studies. (In a later chapter, we will deal with the subject of fasting).

I didn't know I was called to be a healing evangelist. I didn't even know one verse on divine healing! So, I asked Pastor Crager for his help, and he gave me several verses. As youth gathered in the little "Wayside Chapel" to fast and pray, I stood up in front of them and quoted those verses on divine healing and exhorted them to believe God for the girl's healing. Little did I know that I would be quoting those very same verses for decades around the nation and exhorting the sick in church after church to believe God for their healing.

Oh, how many times in my motel before preaching I have quoted to myself (and the devil!) one of those Scriptures the pastor gave me that day:

> **"These signs shall follow them that believe, in My Name. . .they shall lay hands on the sick and they shall recover"** (Mark 16:17, 18). Then I would head for the church with the expectation that the Lord would indeed heal sick bodies.

After a day of fasting and praying, that night after the service, Pastor Crager and we young people gathered around that girl and again prayed. She wasn't healed that night and it was so disappointing. I later learned that the bane of "healing evangelists" would be the many who are prayed over but who do not get healed. The disappointment on people's faces after prayer with no results becomes a humbling motivation repeatedly to keep seeking the Lord, knowing that He alone can do the healing.

Another thing happened that week at camp. A morning class was taught by a LIFE Bible College professor, who would soon become one of my teachers after enrolling at LIFE. He shared with us about Evelyn Thompson, a Foursquare Missionary to the Philippines. She had a great healing ministry. He told the story of how her pet parrot had died, and she picked it up and said, "Now, Lord, You aren't going to let my pet parrot die, are you?" The parrot came back to life!

As the professor told that story, a tear came to my eye. I believe even at that moment the Lord was birthing a healing gift in me. It wouldn't be the last time a tear would come to my eye over sick and dying parrots. . .I mean people.

As a young Christian and then as a young preacher from time to time I would pray for a sick person, but never saw them healed. I remember in one service helping someone pray for a man in a wheelchair. We lifted him out of the chair, trying to encourage him to walk. Momentarily, he turned to us and said, "It hurts!" Sadly, we lowered him back into the chair.

That disappointing scene is burned deeply into my memory banks! It didn't take many failures like that until I figured I must not have the gift of healing. I developed a great deal of unbelief in the area of healing the sick. God had to put me through a great school of the Spirit to change that.

Kathryn Kuhlman Lays Hands On Me

During my sophomore year of Bible College, Kathryn Kuhlman, another great healing evangelist, came to speak at Angelus Temple. Kathryn is the same name and spelling as my wife (must have been prophetic!). That evening, February 14, 1968, she preached to a packed three-story auditorium of 5,300 seats. She spoke to a captivated audience about the great price she paid to have her healing ministry. At the altar call time, she asked,

> **"How many of you want a ministry like this, and you are willing to pay any price to have it? Come forward, and I will lay hands on you."**

A fellow Bible College classmate and I, seated on the first floor, halfway back, were the first ones out of our seats. We were the first ones down at the altar. Kathryn first laid her hands on my friend. He was slain of the Spirit (He fell backward to the floor because the power of God fell upon him). She then laid her hands on me. I wasn't slain, but my call to a ministry of healing was confirmed again through another miracle worker like Aimee Semple McPherson, an evangelist named Kathryn Kuhlman.

Not long after that, my classmate was kicked out of the college for committing fornication. I remained in college by the keeping power and the grace of God. Many years later, I would have the joy of using the same slogan that Evangelist Kuhlman used in her ministry as my advertising theme:

"Expect a Miracle"

Angelus Temple, at the very altar where Aimee once performed great miracles, evidenced by what I admired as a teenager in a display case, was the scene where my DNA as a healing evangelist was confirmed and burned even more deeply into my soul, February 14, 1968.

Oh, how I thank God for two God-called women: Aimee Semple McPherson and Kathryn Kuhlman. They helped me discover my call and destiny to heal the sick.

2

Every Believer's Calling

"Believers will be given the power to perform miracles. . .they will place their hands on sick people, and these will get well"
(Mark 16:17, 18 GNT).

Throughout our American history, many evangelists had ministries accompanied by miracles. Along with Aimee Semple McPherson were such giants in the faith as Maria Woodworth-Etter, John Alexander Dowie, John Lake, Stephen Jeffries, Smith Wigglesworth, and Charles Price. These all had died by 1947.

Christian historians consider 1947 as the year that, what came to be called the 'Healing Revival' began. It lasted, with some exceptions, until about 1958. Shortly after the 2nd World War, an army of miracle-working evangelists felt divinely called by God to invade our nation with God's power. During this time, it is estimated that 1000 tent-evangelists were traversing the United States. Profound healings became commonplace, and there were many decisions for Christ.

Some of the most outstanding healing evangelists of that period were Kathryn Kuhlman, Oral Roberts, A.A. Allen, and T.L. Osborn. All of them either have laid hands on me or at least shaken my hand, which is why I never wash my right hand!

I shared in the previous chapter about Kathryn Kuhlman seeking to impart a healing gift to me. I had the privilege of meeting T.L. Osborn at the Tulsa, Oklahoma International Airport about 2005. I attended the last tent crusade held by Oral Roberts in Anaheim, California in 1967. In the late 1960's, A.A. Allen held one of his last tent crusades in the Los Angeles area. I also visited Allen's tent, along with some of the teenagers from my youth group.

After we got in Allen's prayer line and he laid his hands on us, we danced around the altar area. I am not sure if it was the Holy Spirit motivating us or the excitement a sawdust trail expert could generate, but there we were, our small contribution added to a fading glory. Two of the biggest tents in the history of evangelism, Oral Robert's and A.A. Allen's, were soon folded at last. But I was a part of their history!

During this healing revival, many played their part in this great Holy Ghost demonstration. You may recognize some of their names: William Branham, Tommy Hicks, Kenneth Hagin, A.C. Valdez, Jack Coe, Velmer Gardner, Gayle Jackson, David Duplessis, Raymond Richey, Clifton Erickson, Morris Cerullo, David Nunn, W.V. Grant, Jack Moore, Gordon Lindsay, and Paul Cain, some of the better known at the time. It would be a worthy project to write in this book about every one of them, but I would just be rehashing what has been reported many times before. I have biographies of many of them in my office library. You can google their names and read about the miracles in their ministries if you want to be inspired as I was.

I began reading biographies of those with miracle ministries while I was still a teenager, and I was deeply inspired by their reports. I remember talking with one of my professors at Bible college and telling him that I wouldn't be satisfied until I preached to stadiums full of people. He mentioned how idealistic I was. Well, one man's idealism is another man's vision!

Fasting For The Power

One thing that seemed to be a consistent thread in the lives of all the evangelists' biographies I read was the critical part that fasting played in their lives. Perhaps they found inspiration from David's words in Psalm 35:13:

> **"But as for me, when they were sick, My clothing was sackcloth; I humbled myself with fasting"** (Psalm 35:13).

Much of the fasting by evangelists during the Healing Revival is credited to a book written by Franklin Hall, called *Atomic Power with God, Thru Fasting and Prayer.* It is still available today at Amazon.com. That book helped convince this young preacher to fast like other evangelists had!

So, as soon as I graduated from Bible College, I began a water-only fast to seek God for His power in my life. On the ninth day of the fast, I went up to Camp Cedar Crest to seek the Lord's face at the very place where I first felt the call to ministry.

I walked around, prayed, and meditated among the surrounding forest and hiked once again the trail to the little Wayside Chapel where I had for my first time, fasted, and prayed. I recalled exhorting fellow-seekers to believe God for His healing power to be demonstrated in a teenage girl's life.

I relived again my precious memories of the camp where it all began.

Eventually, I headed back down the hill to where I lived with my parents in Ontario, California. As I drove, I noticed a market and thought I would stop and just, you know, kind of admire the food. As I walked the aisles, my mouth watering, I came upon some free samples. I picked up a couple of the toothpicks holding a tantalizing piece of meat and walked around a while. Trying to resist the urge, time and again, I put my nose close and took a whiff. Ah, the appealing savor to a body starving to death! Of course, you know what happened. I gulped the sample down! My "prophet's fast" now officially over, I bought more food and headed down the hill.

At twenty-one years of age, I had apparently failed at paying the necessary price for the 1947-1958 healing mantle to fall upon my shoulders. There would be other opportunities to fast, many.

After Kathy and I had been married a year, and after a season serving as youth ministers at the Foursquare Church in Crescent City, California, the Lord opened the door for my first pastorate in Sheridan, Wyoming. I was only twenty-three. It was Saturday night before my first Sunday service when I sat playing the piano in the sanctuary. I remember thinking to myself:

"Yes, any day now I will have one of the biggest churches in the Foursquare organization!"

Why? Because Dea Warford had come to town, why do you think?! I was proud, self-confident, and figured with my preaching skills, "great wisdom," and winsome ways my church would grow quickly. However, it didn't take long to discover that the people in Sheridan, Wyoming, could care less that Dea Warford had come to town. In fact, instead of growing, the church began to shrink!

While preaching on a midweek service to a small crowd, I counted five people who were sleeping as I spoke (this wasn't what I wanted to be when I grew up!)!

Where was the power? Where were the miracles? I had read the biographies. I knew what I (thought) I had to do, so I started fasting and praying. I often prayed over a list of things I wanted the Lord to do for me during that fast. Near the top of the list was my desire that God would give me a healing ministry.

I had read biographies of healing evangelists who had gone on long fasts and had visions or angelic appearances. I was hoping an angel would also appear to me and say something like, "Yeah, my son, God has heard your prayer. You'll pull people out of wheelchairs. You'll preach to stadiums full." But nothing like that happened. About the only apparent thing that happened on that fast (besides the hunger and weakness I experienced!) was one day when God gave me a deep desire to do something . . .

The NEAT Team

The Sheridan church was in what was then called, "The Northwest District of Foursquare Churches." At that very season, a group of maybe eight to ten youth was traveling around the district holding crusades in the churches. They called themselves, "The NEAT Team". NEAT was an acronym for the "Northwest Evangelistic Action Team." A young preacher and his wife led the troop.

Still fasting, and during a quiet time in my bedroom, I suddenly had a desire to lead that team. The desire soon passed, and I thought little more about it. A few weeks after my fast was completed, the divisional superintendent told me that the District Supervisor, Dr. Roy Hicks, was coming to the area and wanted to talk to me about something. He wouldn't divulge what it was.

My sister, Elaine, who was living with us at the time and helping me as my "Christian Education Director," and my wife Kathy and I were discussing what Dr. Hicks could possibly want to talk with me about. We figured it must be about taking the pastorate of the Casper, Wyoming church whose pastor we heard was resigning. Excited about a change, we hopped in the car and drove two hours to Casper. The pastor showed us around the church, and we drove around town. I had tired of my ministry at Sheridan and was anxious for change. This was surely it!

However, when Dr. Hicks visited our church and spoke, as we sat together at lunch, he shocked us all! He explained that he wanted the three of us to help lead the next year's NEAT Team. The district would provide a trailer for Kathy and me to live in, a suburban truck to pull it, and we would park the trailer next to the churches where I was speaking. My sister was the counselor for the five girls on the team. A man, a few years their senior, was the counselor of the four boys.

What an adventure! The team had prayer and Bible studies during the mornings. I would lead some of those studies and sometimes the pastor of the church would. In the afternoons, the youth would go door to door or to the local high school to invite people to the services. We formed a choir and had a very talented soloist and guitarist. After they sang, I would preach. We saw many come to Christ during that fruitful time of evangelism in a five-state area (Oregon, Washington, Idaho, Montana, and Wyoming) September-June, 1973-74 tour.

While preaching at those crusades I also saw the healing ministry to which God had called me finally birthed. I began to call the sick forward for prayer, as my predecessors had done so faithfully for generations. This was a real step of faith for me, but the Lord had prepared me for it.

Shortly after that fast at my pastorate in Wyoming, the Lord led me to a booklet by Kenneth Hagin. He was an evangelist and a great faith teacher. I think the title was, *The Authority of the Believer.* Before I read that book, I always thought you had to have an extraordinary gift, a divine impartation, or a vision to begin the operation of divine healing. Kenneth Hagin taught just the opposite. He wrote that Christians don't need some special gift or anointing to heal the sick. All they had to do was use their believer's authority.

Hagin quoted such verses as Mark 16:17, 18:

"These signs shall follow THEM THAT BELIEVE . . .

(notice it doesn't say mighty, powerful evangelists who have had angelic visitations!)

. . . **"they** . . . (that is believers!)

. . . **shall** . . . (not can't or shouldn't!)

. . . **lay hands on the sick and they shall recover."**

In retrospect, I find it interesting that this verse was one of the first verses on divine healing I had learned and taught others at youth camp! Hagin's truth became my truth. I'm hoping my truth will now become your truth!

While on the NEAT Team tour, for the first time in my life, I started calling the sick forward and laying hands on them, commanding them in Jesus' name to be healed. Not all were healed, and we didn't see great miracles, but people began to regularly testify of receiving a healing touch. I thus became not only a soul-winning evangelist but a traditional "healing evangelist" as well.

My life would never be the same. Your life will never be the same either if you'll just start acting like a Bible-believer.

You are a believer, aren't you? If so, then you have a calling to:

> **"Lay hands on the sick and they shall recover."**

3

Old Eccentric Evangelist

**"God has chosen the foolish things of the world
to put to shame the wise, and God has chosen
the weak things of the world to put to shame
the things which are mighty"**
(1 Corinthians 1:27).

That God would choose a man such as I to a miracle ministry demonstrates the above truth. At one time, I was so full of unbelief when it came to divine healing that I can remember a service I was in where someone had a cold. I'm not exaggerating; I purposely tried to stay on the opposite side of the sanctuary from where they were lest they should ask me to pray for their cold! I was indeed one of "the weak things of the world" mentioned above.

Then, there was my sin. I struggled with pride, jealousy, lust, and trivial worldly pursuits. Though I pastored and even held revivals sometimes, from 1974-1981, I tried to avoid praying for the sick. I was full of condemnation for my sin. I felt I was an unclean vessel. Ministering miracles is very demanding. It is embarrassing when you pray for someone, and they aren't healed, especially if you are filled with pride to begin with!

I would play the piano and sing in services (showing off my talents!). I would teach Christians how to win souls. I would preach some good sermons. (At least I sure thought they were good!). But then, after preaching, out of habit, out of a sense of duty (after all, God called me to be a healing evangelist!), I would tell the congregation:

"Does anybody need healing? If so, come up to the front now, and I'll pray for you."

When nobody came forward, inside, I was relieved, silently thinking to myself, "Whew! That's a relief!" Healings were not happening through me and, though the Lord did use me to help win souls to Christ and a few other helpful things, I was nevertheless guilty of violating Paul's word in 1 Timothy 1:14:

"Do not neglect the gift that is in you."

Like many other evangelists before me, I was living way below my privileges and rights as both a son of God and as a miracle worker.

I attended a meeting where Evangelist Maurice Martin was speaking. He taught on faith and healing, and then he invited the people to help him pray for the sick. He was an older man, about eighty, but had a reputation for healing the sick. John DeLorean, the engineer, inventor, and automobile executive, had been healed of heart problems through Brother Martin's prayers. John was the one who invented the DMC sports car featured in the 1985 film *Back to the Future* (the healing lasted since John didn't die until 2005 of a stroke at eighty years old!).

In that service, Evangelist Martin called people forward who were in any kind of pain. That evangelist was so eccentric (most evangelists are!). He would be talking with a person about the nature and location of the pain and then suddenly, without warning, would jump towards them (like in a horror movie!) and shout, "GO!!!!!" If they didn't pass out from fright, many testified of healing.

Then Evangelist Martin did something I had never seen an evangelist do. He asked for laypeople from the audience to pray for others who were in pain. He even had one person come to the platform and pray for someone who had already come forward for prayer. This old and experienced evangelist believed that anyone could expect a miracle to happen through their prayers, a fact that would soon dramatically change my ministry.

Desperate For The Power

**"You will seek Me and you will find Me,
when you search for Me with all your heart"**
(Jeremiah 29:13).

In November of 1981, I became desperate for the power and to see healings again in my evangelistic meetings. I thus determined to fast my breakfast for forty days until the power to heal returned. I told myself if that didn't do the trick, I would try something else. I was determined! With my fast metabolism, I am ready to eat my breakfast about as soon as my feet hit the floor in the morning, so it was a significant decision and sacrifice.

I would seek the Lord those mornings. We were living with my parents at the time so, for privacy, I would drive out a few miles to a row of eucalyptus trees, paralleling an old farm road. I would pace and pray, and then I would sit in my car and read the word. I would walk the area again and pray some more. I would eat a banana at about 11 AM to break my fast before eating lunch at about noon.

I had been doing this for maybe two or three weeks when on a Sunday morning during the fast, I drove an hour to minister in a small church in Cabazon, California. In the audience that morning sat Evangelist Maurice Martin. I had no idea why he was sitting there listening to me, but I appreciated it. When it was time for the altar call, I said,

"Those of you who want to get right with God, need deliverance or the baptism in the Holy Spirit, I will be standing here at the left side of the altar to pray for you. If you need healing, Brother Martin is here this morning, and He has the gift of healing. I am going to ask him to come up and stand on the right side of the altar, and if you are sick, he will be happy to pray for you."

I imagine the people thought, "That sure is humble of Dea to do that." Humble? Are you kidding? I was just tickled to have someone else to handle the hard cases!

That same week, Evangelist Martin gave me a phone call. He lived about twenty miles from me, and said he wanted to come over and talk. I was happy to visit with him. As we sat in the living room, He revealed the reason for coming. He told me:

"Dea, you don't need some healing gift to heal the sick. All you need to do is use your believer's authority."

(Where had I heard that before?). I listened politely, but I really didn't see his counsel as the answer to my prayers. I went right back to my prayer spot the next day and cried out again, "God restore to me my healing ministry!"

A Healing Ministry Restored

Within a week or two, I was scheduled to teach a congregation in Granada Hills on principles of personal evangelism (my book *EVANGELIST* teaches many of these same principles of soul-winning). The first service, as I sat on the platform with the pastor, he did something I have never seen done before or since. He approached the pulpit and announced: "My wife and I want to pray for everybody here this morning. Please line up to the left and come to the front."

I remained seated on the platform, observing the pastor's entire congregation leaving their seats to receive prayer. Comfortably waiting for my turn, the Holy Spirit unexpectedly spoke to my heart and said:

"If you will pray for the sick tonight, I will heal them."

Huh? I was at that very moment watching the pastor praying for everybody in the church. I was to have the gall to announce to everybody: "Now that the pastor prayed for you, and nothing happened, how about letting a real man of God get his hands on you!" I couldn't do that! It was his church and I was but a guest. But then, it came to me again: "If you will pray for the sick tonight, I will heal them."

I thought about it a moment and suddenly got a brainstorm! After the pastor introduced me, I came to the pulpit and simply said:

"When the pastors were praying for you, they weren't praying specifically for your physical healing. But I believe the Lord has spoken to me that if I pray for the sick, He will heal you today. I want everybody who is experiencing pain in your body (that's how the other eccentric evangelist, Brother Martin did it!) to form a line to my left." Oh, was that ever a sick church! A line maybe twenty-five or thirty deep approached me (what had I gotten myself into?!).

When the first man stood before me on the platform, I asked, "Where is your pain?" He said, "I have pain in my stomach." (was I glad it wasn't cerebral palsy!). I laid hands on him and then boldly and with authority said, "In the name of Jesus, I command this pain to leave!" Then I asked him, "Where is the pain?" He replied, "It's gone!" (Hallelujah! One down, twenty-nine to go!)

The next person in line told me they had pain in their back. I laid hands on the back and commanded the pain to leave. "Where is the pain now?" I asked. "It's gone!" he replied.

Not everyone received healing in that church that day. However, enough people testified of a healing touch that I knew (and the devil knew!) that I was back in the healing business. I began having prayer lines again in my services.

In many churches, I would ask those who were in pain to stand to their feet where they were seated. Then after a brief teaching on the authority of the believer and how to pray against pain, I would ask other believers in the congregation to get out of their seats and lay hands on someone who had pain in their body (again, imitating the old evangelist).

I used this method around America. God is my witness; there are many churches where after doing this, without me even laying a hand on a sick body, a line of people would approach the front and testify into the microphone of a miracle of healing. Many who had been in long-term high levels of pain testified of either feeling the pain completely gone or substantially subsided. I have personally witnessed it around the nation. In fact, just as many people are healed if their fellow church members pray for them than if the "big-gun" evangelist prays for them (and this is a personally witnessed fact!).

The authority of the believer over sickness was Evangelist Maurice Martin's truth. Now that truth had once again, as years previously, become my truth. And I trust after finishing this book, your authority as a believer to pray for the sick will become your truth as well.

I needed an old eccentric evangelist named Brother Martin to help stir me up to fulfill my destiny. Let an eccentric Evangelist named Dea help stir you up to fulfill your destiny!

Read on, you healing evangelist you!

4

The Ghost of Healing Evangelists Past

"Now all these things happened to them as examples, and they were written for our admonition, on whom the end of the ages have come" (1 Corinthians 10:12).

I have seen the ghost of healing evangelists past. Though now dead, I learned a lot from them.

Older readers can remember when churches would have several "revivals" a year with a guest evangelist. Meetings would run a week or sometimes weeks long, every night, maybe with one night dark for rest (for everybody!).

In those days, just about anybody with a traveling ministry would be referred to as an "evangelist"— musicians, singers, puppeteers, even retired pastors who wanted to continue to preach a bit. Some called themselves "evangelist" who weren't, and some who called themselves something else (like "pastor, teacher, psalmist," etc.) were actually evangelists. Of course, the gift isn't a title; it is an anointing and a divine calling.

During the 1947-1958 healing revival, God called men and women from every walk of life to become evangelists. Some stayed faithful until the end, and others fell; some fell hard!

An Evangelist Turned Pastor

Rudy Cerullo was among those working miracles during the healing revival. He was featured in Gordon Lindsay's Voice of Healing magazine. You can google Evangelist Rudy Cerullo and see his posters, but don't confuse him with his son, still living, who has the same name.

I preached in 2002 for Rudy in Covina, California, where he was pastoring an Assembly of God Church. He was an older man by then. Rudy, like so many other evangelists, had to leave the sawdust trail and pastor a church after the anointing for that season of revival had lifted.

Rudy had a small crowd of people. His wife was in a wheelchair, as I recall. The pastor told me how one of his board members could hardly believe the stories he told him of the miracles Rudy had seen in his years as an essential actor in the history of evangelism in America. I don't remember much about that day, but I was tickled when Rudy told me that I reminded him of one of the greats of the healing revival, T.L. Osborn!

Evangelist A.A. Allen

Evangelist A.A. Allen had one of the greatest healing ministries of all time. His protégé, the late R.W. Shambach, followed in his steps. I was in one of R.W.'s tent crusades in Pomona, California, before he passed on to his reward. I have listened to many of R.W.'s sermons on YouTube. He is one of my favorite evangelists.

R.W. tells the story of a woman who brought her little son to one of Allen's meetings. The boy had been born with twenty-six diseases. He couldn't see, hear, or speak. His limbs were crippled and deformed and he had club feet. Though four years old, he had never walked. The Lord gave Allen a word of knowledge as Allen described seeing (in the Spirit) a baby with 26 diseases and called up the mother. She ran up to the platform with the boy in her arms.

Allen told everyone to close their eyes while he prayed, but R.W. said he wasn't about to miss seeing this miracle! Before his eyes, R.W. saw the boy's limbs snap into place. The boy could see, talk and walk for the first time. There is no doubt that A.A. Allen had an anointing for miracles.

In May of 2011, I held a revival at the Palominos, Arizona, Assembly of God Church. During the day, my sister, Elaine, and I drove over to nearby "Miracle Valley." (The title defines its history). The property comprised over a thousand acres which A.A. had purchased in 1958, at the tail-end of the healing revival. He built a good-sized cathedral on it and a Bible College.

People would come from all over America with tents and trailers to camp out on the property and be a part of the ongoing healing and deliverance crusades that Allen and his staff held there. Allen tried hard to keep the healing revival fires fanned but died in 1970 at the age of 59. I feel privileged to have seen him in person just months before he died.

My sister and I parked our rental car, climbed a rickety barbed wire fence, and wandered around the property for a while. Weeds grew everywhere. The cathedral had broken doors so that we could walk around inside. Windows were broken, pieces of the ceiling had fallen to the floor. It looked like it hadn't had services for decades and was not being maintained. It was sad and haunting. The healing revival was officially over.

The Gospel Tent

The thousand gospel tents of the 1950s, often filled with hundreds or even thousands, had dwindled to a tent set up here and there, sometimes with but a handful of people inside, evangelists and saints seeking to relive bygone glory days. I have preached in a few of those tents myself.

In the late 1960s, Evangelist Bob Herald let me preach one night in a tent he had set up on an empty field in the Riverside, California area. Maybe twenty or so, if that, were there that night.

When I pastored a church in Hawaiian Gardens before I launched on the evangelistic field, I did a lot of research about tents. I just knew I could resurrect a tent crusade! I solicited the city to let us utilize an undeveloped piece of property for an old-fashioned evangelistic crusade (starring me, of course! Oh. . . and the Holy Spirit!).

The city attorney convinced the mayor that the city would be liable if anything happened. My dream was shattered. I found it interesting that not long after that, they allowed a traveling circus to set up THEIR tent in the city. I guess a lawsuit by someone for being stomped by an elephant would be less expensive than someone suing an evangelist for pushing them over with the power . . . of his right arm!

I longed for many years to one day have my own tent and have old-fashioned healing crusades, like those I had witnessed in my youth. Then, in the summer of 2000, the Butte, Montana Foursquare Church gave me the privilege of being their evangelist for a tent crusade (could this be the start of my destiny?). I was so excited that I took my wife and two children, Carissa, and Nathan, with me to witness this.

The pastor told me on the phone where the tent would be set up, near downtown. We flew in, rented a car, and wanted to see this future historic site right away. We drove up and down the streets, trying to find it. When we did, it was not a tent, but several chintzy-looking plastic tarps set up in a vacant parking lot with folding chairs underneath. My heart sank. My family saw my disappointment and felt so sorry for me. (I don't know why the Lord always picks on me as a favorite subject of humbling. It surely couldn't be because I need it!)

Despite the disappointment and relatively small crowds, God showed up, and good things happened. I ministered in one more tent set up by two Foursquare Churches in Salina, Kansas, that same summer. And that was it.

The days of the gospel tent may be forever over, at least in the U.S.A. or at least for me. Why is that? Perhaps we could blame evangelists' sensationalism. Then there were the money raising shenanigans. The fading display of supernatural power was surely a very big factor too. As an evangelist, I want to blame pampered saints who aren't willing to make the effort! Then, there were increasingly stringent city planning, fire safety regulations, and high costs of insurance. There were doubtless many contributing factors. Alas!

A slowly dying off generation of those who still remember the good old days when the Gospel Tent was king (as I can!) take their memories with them. That's one reason I am writing this book! I want to keep the memory alive. But, of course, we don't need more of the tents today nearly as much as we need more of the power! At one time a gospel tent was a lodestone for both saint and sinner to come out and see a gospel circus clown, I mean, evangelist, and maybe a miracle or two.

Times change, much to the sorrow of this evangelist. To show how closely my heart is entwined with Gospel Tents, I told my wife that if I die on one of my revivals in another state, to save the expense of shipping my body back home, and instead have me cremated. Then have someone scatter my ashes among the sawdust in some gospel tent, if there are any left!

Through the years, when I heard of evangelists holding crusades, I would often go to hear and see them. I wanted to see the miracles, and I wanted to learn the tricks of the trade.

A Fallen Assembly of God Evangelist

Around 1970, an evangelist I'll call C.E. held a many weeks' long revival, I think 11 weeks, at an Assembly of God Church not far from where I lived at the time. I attended several services. He had an unusual anointing. Almost everybody he prayed for was "slain of the Spirit" (or as some call it, "fell under the power," or "rested in the Spirit.").

People would line up in the aisles to be prayed for and the evangelist would walk through the church laying hands on each one. I had never seen anything quite like it. When he prayed for me, I didn't fall (I have never fallen under the power. I used to think it was because I was so full of power! Oh, what a proud young man I was!).

My father, Paul, was with me during a service. He was backslidden at the time, yet he still enjoyed going to a good service. As bodies piled up in the aisle, he later told me that he had thought to himself, "Well, this is nice that these people are experiencing this, but I won't be falling." As the evangelist laid hands on him, he immediately fell to the floor! Even unbelievers who came to arrest Christ fell under the power in John 18:6:

> **"Now when He said to them, "I am He," they drew back and fell to the ground."**

This falling under the power phenomenon helped Evangelist C.E. fill churches night after night and he preached in some of the biggest Assembly of God churches in America. I still have a copy of his newsletter from 1973 with testimonies of miracles in his ministry. Then, abruptly, he was accused of homosexuality. The district examined the evidence; he lost his license with the Assemblies.

Soon, his ministry dwindled and the last time I saw him he was preaching in a little Pentecostal church in Ontario where I had preached several times.

I met Evangelist C.E. in the foyer, where I noticed as he talked to me, he kept blinking with one eye. I gave him the benefit of the doubt (maybe it was just an eye-twitch?). Later the pastor of the church where he had spoken that night resigned and began pastoring a gay-affirming church. How could he do that? He was a good pastor! We had been friends for many years. Then, when I heard that the pastor died from AIDS, I began putting all the pieces together.

> **"The gifts and calling of God are irrevocable"**
> (Romans 11:29)

The fallen evangelist continued to minister through the years. Not long ago, when I went to his Facebook page, there was a picture of him in what looked like a Catholic Cardinal's uniform, with the chess-piece type of tall, pointed hat. It looked ridiculous for a Pentecostal preacher. He referred to himself no longer as Evangelist but as "Bishop!"

The Lord only knows how his doctrines may have evolved through the years or if he too became a gay-affirming preacher. I think he is dead now. I hope he made it through! What a loss for the church! And what a warning to those who desire to see miracles to live a holy life.

Evangelist Leroy Jenkins

My sister and I attended Evangelist Leroy Jenkins' revival in an auditorium in San Bernardino, California, about 1970. Leroy used a secular rock & roll band as his "worship" team. That night they even performed the famous song "Raindrops Keep Falling on my Head." Leroy, to our shock and stupefaction, referring to his band, said, "These men live cleaner lives than most Christians." The band members smiled proudly.

Then Jenkins had Mae West come to the platform. Mae was by then an aged Hollywood Starlet who first starred in a Broadway play in 1926 which she had written, produced, and directed, called *Sex*. She was arrested and given ten days in jail for "corrupting the morals of youth." Mae became a sex-symbol of her time, long before Marilyn Monroe came along.

That an evangelist would have someone like that standing with him on the platform was unprecedented! In her Burlesque queenly outfit, she addressed the wide-eyed audience, repeating her famous line, "It's not the men in your life that counts. It's the life in your men!"

As though that weren't enough, Leroy announced, "I will pray for you and God will heal you if you will give $100.00 to my ministry." Some desperate people fell for the line and went forward. Of course, we were stunned by such a statement!

Evangelist Jenkins eventually served time in prison on charges of conspiracy to commit arson and assault. He filed for bankruptcy and was indicted for tax evasion. He also was accused of selling contaminated "Miracle Water." Leroy Jenkins died in 2017, but his ghost haunts the reputation of healing evangelists even today.

Nationally Known Televangelists

Televangelist Jim Baker's over-selling of timeshares sent him to prison for mail fraud, wire fraud, and conspiracy. Also, about this time, his motel room encounter with a woman named Jessica Hahn made him the laughingstock of Hollywood. The media had a field day with what they felt was incontrovertible evidence of the hypocrisy of evangelical Christianity. Jim was sentenced to 45 years in prison. Thank God, he was released early, restored to the body of Christ and now has a wonderful television ministry once again.

Jimmy Swaggart was another televangelist. He was at one time on 3,000 TV stations in America and foreign countries. His piano playing, singing, and preaching made him a favorite of many sinners. In the late 1980s, Jimmy began ranting on his television shows about the sins of other preachers.

I read something revealing in his national newsletter called *The Evangelist*. In it, Jimmy claimed that his ministry was:

"The greatest evangelistic ministry in the world."

I remember wincing when I read that statement that seemed to wreak with pride. Evelyn Thompson, a retired missionary, commented concerning Jimmy that, "He either has already fallen or he is going to fall." As Proverbs 16:18 warns,

"Pride goes before destruction, And a haughty spirit before a fall."

Soon came photographic proof of Swaggart having a rendezvous in a motel with a prostitute. Then, for a second time, he was filmed cavorting with another prostitute! Thus Jimmy was soon defrocked by the Assemblies of God.

On national television, he repented with his now famous,"I have sinned!" admission. I watched that played and replayed again and again by secular television, mocking evangelical Christianity, and reveling in our "hypocrisy." Even a number of Rock and Roll songs were written to make fun of Jimmy's fall.

Jimmy Swaggart Bible College, which had over 1400 students, declined to only 400 or so. Swaggart also lost many radio and television stations. Yet, the worst thing that resulted from all this, was the loss of the reputation of the body of Christ.

My cousin, who had a church and children's school and mission station in Belize, said that after Jimmy's debacle, her donations went down 40%. What in the world did one man's sin have to do with ministering to needy children in a foreign country?! My late brother, Ed, who was unsaved at the time, told me:

"I can understand the prostitute. Jimmy is just flesh (Ed pinched the flesh of his arm while saying this)**, but the hypocrisy!"**

Surely when evangelists fall, this causes a fulfillment of Scripture:

"A righteous man falling down before the wicked is as a troubled fountain, and a corrupt spring" (Proverbs 25:26 KJV).

When Jimmy's fall was being shouted from the housetops, I remember being so thankful that the Lord had delivered me from pornography! Years later, when I was again in full-time evangelistic ministry, after settling for a few minutes in my Motel 6 room, I heard a knock on the door. It was a prostitute who had seen me arrive. She said through the door, "Would you like some company in there?" I said, "No! I would like to get some sleep."

Though I have said and done many foolish things in my decades of evangelism, at least (thank God!) I haven't lost my ministry because I have fallen morally.

Many evangelists have fallen because of women. Others fall because of money, or pride. One evangelist from the "Healing Revival" confessed, "I know I will never make heaven my home because I love money and women too much." Other evangelists have not fallen from grace, but they have fallen out of favor with man.

Televangelist Peter Popoff

I personally witnessed Televangelist Peter Popoff's "fall." He had what appeared to be a dramatic and unusual word of knowledge gift. In his services he would call out names, addresses, and conditions of people and then pray for them.

I was in a service where he was calling names out. In a theatrical style, he would say something like, "Judy? Judy Thompson? Where are you? Stand up Judy!" Then he would either come to them and lay hands on them or pronounce them healed.

I was thrilled at first as I watched this fantastic demonstration of supernatural knowledge. Then my heart suddenly sank! I could not help but notice that out of a large audience of people, maybe a thousand, that there were too many who just "happened" to be sitting in the first row or so of the balcony. The odds of probability, at least to my mathematical mind, would not account for that high number when so many more were sitting on the first floor.

It wasn't long after that that skeptics with electronic equipment visited one of Popoff's services and were able to intercept radio transmissions coming from his wife. Popoff would wear a receiver in his ear as she would call out names and other information for him to repeat. These "supernatural facts" apparently had been gleaned from visitor's cards filled out before the service.

Popoff was exposed on national television when one of the skeptics provided Johnny Carson with incontrovertible audio taped evidence of Popoff's deception. Much damage resulted from this revelation and Popoff had to file bankruptcy. His reputation was badly tarnished.

Eventually, though, Popoff regained his television ministry and is worth millions today. Some think that Steve Martin borrowed from Peter Popoff in his 1992 movie *Leap of Faith* and Chevy Chase did the same in his movie *Fletch Lives.* When evangelists don't judge themselves, the world, through the media, is happy to do so.

All of the above evangelists may have truly repented and are now relaxing in their heavenly mansion or on earth, walking with the Lord in integrity. I am not judging them. The things I write are nevertheless true, and most of these things are common knowledge. David committed murder and adultery, which became common knowledge, yet God said of Him:

> **"I have found David the son of Jesse, a man after mine own heart, which shall fulfill all my will"** (Acts 13:22 KJV).

I trust that any past sins of the above evangelists are under the blood. God knows I have my share of sins that I would hate to have been brought up by the media! Still, I have learned from other evangelists' mistakes. Not wanting to see my ministry end in ill-repute, I long ago prayed:

> **"God, if you see I am about to commit adultery, kill me first!"**

And I have had God answer enough prayers to believe He would do it too! And my wife said, "If God doesn't kill you, I will!" So, I'm in big trouble any way you look at it!

Satan is very aware that miracles attract crowds, and crowds coming out to hear the gospel is a significant threat to his kingdom. Thus, he fought the healing revival and will still today contend against any evangelist or layman who seeks to see God's power displayed for the world to see.

Satan saw the potential in Peter as Jesus had when he called him to be an apostle. The devil went after the Apostle Peter just as he went after the above evangelists. Jesus was aware of Satan's scheme, and so He warned Peter:

> **"Simon, Simon! Indeed, Satan has asked for you, that he may sift you as wheat. But I**

**have prayed for you, that your faith should
not fail; and when you have returned to Me,
strengthen your brethren"** (Luke 22:32).

Please pray for me. I am but one among a steady historical stream of evangelists, many of whom are now ghosts. Pray that my faith will not fail and that my feet will stay planted firmly on the Rock. Pray also that I will spend the rest of my days preaching, praying, and writing books like this one to "strengthen (my) brethren."

A Final Warning to us all from Paul the Apostle

I think the Message Bible translation puts it best:

**"These are all warning markers - danger! - in
our history books, written down so that we
don't repeat their mistakes. Our positions in
the story are parallel - they at the beginning,
we at the end - and we are just as capable
of messing it up as they were. Don't be so
naive and self-confident. You're not exempt.
You could fall flat on your face as easily as
anyone else"** (1 Corinthians 10:11, 12 MSG).

5

Oral Roberts

"The king said to his officers, "Don't you know that today a leader, a great man, has fallen in Israel?" (2 Samuel 3:38 GW).

Evangelist Oral Roberts (b. 1/24/1918, d. 12/15/2009) influenced my life when I was a young man feeling the call to be an evangelist. I met him while working at the Full Gospel Business Men's Fellowship office in downtown Los Angeles. It was about 1967.

While doing janitorial-type work that day, as I walked down the hall, I was met by my boss and another man. "Dea," said my boss, "I'd like you to meet Oral Roberts."

I reached out to shake the hand of the tall evangelist, with no idea at the time how much his life would influence mine.

No one would have to ask me, as a king in 2 Samuel asked above: "Don't you know that today a leader, a great man, has fallen in Israel?" I know Oral was a "leader" and "a great man." Let me explain why I genuinely believe that.

We all revered Evangelist Billy Graham. But what many don't know is that at one time, Oral Roberts was the 2nd most recognized name in USA religion, second only to Billy Graham.

Evangelist Oral Roberts left behind quite a legacy . . .

- ORU, "Oral Roberts University," in Tulsa, OK (I lived about six miles from it for over a year, 2005-2006. I even watched my son, Nathan, receive his high school diploma in a ceremony at ORU's Maybee Center, an 11,300 seat arena).

- Oral wrote 133 books.

- Thousands were saved and many healed through his ministry.

- Oral was one of the first to pioneer national crusades brought into homes through television.

- He preached to some of the largest crowds of his time, even into the tens of thousands.

- Oral at one time had the world's largest Gospel Tent.

- He was also one of the first "televangelists" (starting in 1954); within a year, he was on over 200 stations! Later, His prime-time TV program became the most-viewed religious program in America.

Oral helped launch the FGBMFI or "Full Gospel Business Men's Fellowship International" (I worked for its headquarters in the 60's when I was in Bible College in Los Angeles). The FGBMFI was an organization that helped fan the flames of the "charismatic movement," a move of God that began in the '60s. This movement brought mainline denominations and even some Catholics into things the "wrong side of the tracks"

Pentecostals had experienced for many years—divine healing, tongues, prophecy, and other works of the Holy Spirit.

Oral's life was a great inspiration to me when I was a young preacher. I read and reread his autobiography to challenge myself. I learned from his experiences working with the Holy Spirit. His life bore witness that each of us has a destiny and an important task to fulfill during our time on earth. Oral Roberts was known for being restless and driven. That restlessness that you may feel today could be nothing less than your spirit longing for the timing and the power to fulfill your destiny.

Oral also felt he had a divine calling on his life. Do you sense what your calling is? I have had, since high school, a life-long sense of divine calling. I have had many fulfilling experiences in serving God, but I know there is more God wants to do through me. Do you sense that there is more that God wants to do through you? This is a primary reason God led me to write this book you are reading.

Let's all, like Elisha, grab hold of Oral's "mantle" and pray Elisha's prayer,

"Where is the God of Elijah?" (2 Kings 2:14).

We might also ask, "Where is the God of Oral?" May the clear mandate that Elijah and men like Oral Roberts had (which empowered their life) also become our own mandate from God!

Despite his advanced age, Oral continued ministering until his last public appearance three months before his passing in 2009.

I was surprised (I shouldn't have been) that in the face of the significant influence of Oral's life, neither CNN nor FOX news network made mention of his passing the morning after Oral's death (yet, oh, what a big deal they made from "Playboy Magazine" founder Hugh Hefner's passing!). The world barely noticed Oral's disappearance from this planet. Yet, the thousands who escaped hell through his preaching surely gave him a celebratory greeting in heaven!

I've learned from Oral's difficult lessons. For instance, after seeing how the world responded to some of his public announcements, I'll try to be careful before I make bold claims of visions or hearing the voice of God (not that I don't believe in them, only that Oral's experience proves how readily the world will reject them anyway!).

For example, Oral once claimed that he saw a vision of a 900-foot-tall Jesus. The world mocked him for that. Signs were posted around Tulsa, his hometown, which read, "900-foot-tall Jesus Crossing."

I try to be careful in my finances and lifestyle as an evangelist (not that I have enough money for anybody to accuse me of charlatanism! If they accuse me of poverty ...). Oral claimed that the Lord told him that if he didn't raise enough money to finish his medical center that God was going to "take him home." This "word" seemed ridiculous to the world, and only scare tactics, and sensationalism befitting a televangelist.

Thank God, at least Oral was never accused of sexual indiscretions.

We all have our strengths and weaknesses. We all have our successes and failings. David was known as a giant killer, but he also was remembered as a murderer and adulterer. How people remember us after our deaths will be determined by what we say and do with our lives. Thus, we surely want to humbly seek

God's help with our weaknesses and strive to use our strengths to do our best for His kingdom.

I have certainly made missteps through the years. I would hate for people to define my worth and my worthiness to be a man of God by these negative things, worthy as they may be of criticism. I hope that they will consider the good things that God has wrought through my life as that which counted, and not dismiss my life as inconsequential because of my errors. Don't you want the same from your life?

Though Oral's ministry wound down over his last few decades and though there was some controversy surrounding his life, at least he completed his mission on earth.

In Second Timothy, Paul the apostle had received a word from the Lord that his journey on earth was about to end. Maybe Oral also received a word from God that helped prepare him for his homecoming. If so, I'm sure that in his last few months, Oral looked back on his life's accomplishments with a measurable sense of fulfillment and joy. Perhaps like Paul writing his final letter to Timothy, Oral also wrote to his son Richard:

> **"The time of my departure is at hand. I have a fought a good fight, I have finished my course, I have kept the faith. Finally, there is laid up for me the crown of righteousness"** (II Timothy 4:6-8).

Oral fought a good fight. He may, like us all, have lost a few rounds, but he nevertheless "won Christ" (Phil. 3:8). He finished the race and kept the faith. And he'll receive his "crown of righteousness," not because he never made mistakes, but for the same reason you and I will receive our crown: because of the righteousness of Christ (II Corinthians 5:21).

Apostle John was an older man when he wrote,

> **"Then I heard a voice from heaven saying to
> me, "Write: 'Blessed are the dead who die in
> the Lord from now on.'"" "Yes," says the Spirit,
> "that they may rest from their labors, and
> their works follow them"** (Revelations 14:13).

Oral lived to be an older man and lived a full and prosperous life. He is now at "rest from (his) labor." His "works follow" him too . . .

- Preachers graduate each year from ORU to preach the gospel around the world.

- Numerous professionals work worldwide who received their education because of Oral Roberts. Their witness for Christ in the marketplace was doubtless greatly influenced by the strong Christian atmosphere established on that campus; the continuing fruitfulness emanating from Oral's obedience to God's word to him when he was but a 17-year-old.

- Evangelists, like me, are challenged to continue the healing, salvation crusades that Oral championed.

- 133 different books are in personal, and public libraries read and reread, inspiring others.

- His son, Richard, now oversees the Oral Roberts Ministries.

- My late brother Ed and his wife, Barbara, wanted children, but they had not been able to conceive. While watching Oral on TV, when Oral instructed those watching to lay their hand on the area that needed healing, Ed laid his hand on Barbara's womb. They went on soon to have the first of three children!

Yes indeed, I think we can safely say, as John said, that Oral Roberts' "works follow him."

Oral's Life On Earth COUNTED!

Oral Roberts was a poor son of a farmer and part-time preacher. As a teen, he was dying of tuberculosis. But, on his way to receive prayer from an evangelist holding a tent crusade, God spoke to Oral and said,

> **"I am going to heal you, and you are to take my healing power to your generation. You are to build me a university and build it on my authority and the Holy Spirit."**

That night in that gospel tent, God healed him and delivered him from a life-long problem with stuttering. He was preaching revivals at the age of 18.

I have personally stood in the little Pentecostal Holiness church where Oral once pastored in Enid, Oklahoma. I knelt and prayed at the altar area where Oral himself prayed in 1947 — the very place where God launched Oral's healing ministry. I stood too in the auditorium in Enid, where Oral preached his first healing crusade and healed the sick in front of a crowd of 1200 people.

Having sought God for a healing ministry much of my adult life, I think I have some idea of what went through Oral's mind many times during his earlier years. I empathize with him as perhaps few reading this can. I believe he was sincere in what He felt was God's call. And, like Paul the apostle, he was:

> **"not disobedient to the heavenly vision"**
> (Acts 26:19).

Take careful note: God called Oral during his youth and told him what He wanted Oral to accomplish with his life. Young person, seek the Lord to discover what God wants you to do with your life. You have your youth, your zeal, your strength, and your vitality. Dedicate your all to His call!

For those of us who are older, tired, and feel life may have already "passed us by," we can find inspiration from, not only Oral, a man who ministered into his 90's, but from Psalm 71:8:

> **"Now also when I am old and gray-headed,**
> **O God, do not forsake me, Until I declare**
> **Your strength to this generation, Your power**
> **to everyone who shall come."**

Oral "declared (God's) strength to (his) generation" as well as God's "power." Now he's gone, but you and I still have the opportunity to declare God's strength to our generation.

Most Americans of our generation have never experienced the power of God. They have never seen a miracle. They have never had a vision, dream, or prophetic word. Many have never heard the "Good News." They need someone, like Oral, to show them the reality of God's power and preach the "good news" to them.

I'm determined, in spite of the fact that I am "old and gray-headed," to be one who declares God's "strength, power," and "good news" to my generation!

Oral's "life mission," which began over a century ago, is over. For some of you, your journey has barely begun. The mantle that was on Oral can now rest on you. Oral once claimed that the power in his life resulted from a certain (supernatural) "strength" that came to him.

You will only be this kind of last days Christian if you learn how to plug into that same supernatural strength. Therefore, let us resolve to seek God's face, as Oral did in 1947, when on his knees for 30 days at mealtimes, with fasting and prayers, he read the Gospels and Acts to discover the key to fulfill his calling. Let us resolve that we might, like Oral Roberts and like the Psalmist, soon claim,

> **"I have been anointed with fresh oil"**
> (Psalm 92:10).

Maybe at this time you aren't burdened, like I am, to have healing power. You're not likely called to have tent crusades or to build a college either. Nevertheless, you still have a unique calling, and it is your responsibility to discover and fulfill that calling:

> **"Wherefore the rather, brethren, give diligence to make your calling and election sure"** (2 Peter 1:10, KJV).

Remember, everyone is called to "do the work of an evangelist" (2 Tim. 4:5). We do this when we endeavor to win souls and heal the sick. Evangelist Oral Roberts did just that for seven decades!

Oral Robert's voice on earth is now silenced. Yours is still sounding! It's up to you to take the baton from Oral's hand and continue the race. Oral's mantle is now (like Elijah's after he went to heaven) resting on the planet earth, still pulsating with power. Who among us dares pick it up?

One final note is the following quote from a website where you can explore more about Oral:

"In 1935, as a young man named Oral Roberts lay dying of incurable tuberculosis in Enid, Oklahoma, the Lord spoke to the young man and said:

> **'Son, I am going to heal you, and you are to take My healing power to your generation. And someday, you are to build Me a university based on My authority and on the Holy Spirit.'**

That very night, Oral's brother drove him to a tent revival in Ada, Oklahoma, where **Evangelist George Moncey** laid his hands on Oral's fevered, weak body and prayed, 'You foul, tormenting disease, I command you in the Name of Jesus Christ of Nazareth, come out of this boy! Loose him and let him go free!'

The power of God hit Oral's body, and he received immediate healing in his lungs, as well as his stuttering tongue." (source: https://oralroberts.com/our-history/)

In bold letters above is the name Evangelist George Moncey, a name you probably didn't recognize. Yet, because of Moncey's faithfulness to obey his "earthly mission" and pray for the sick, thousands were saved and healed and millions were touched by the life of Oral Roberts, who also would have likely remained an unknown without the faithfulness of Evangelist George Moncey!

You think you are an unknown? I believe miracles are your destiny. That truth is already known in heaven. Oral Roberts stands as the epitome of how God can take the weak and make them strong for His purposes. God grant that the life of Oral Roberts, this book, and your hungry spirit will help you discern, lay hold on, and fulfill your destiny:

"As unknown, and *yet* well known.. as poor, yet making many rich; as having nothing, and *yet* possessing all things"
(2 Corinthians 6:9, 10).

May you find great inspiration from the heavenly poem of Oral Roberts' life!

Let's rejoice and stand in awe and expectation of the soon coming glory of God to heal the sick that will fall upon this planet and upon you!

So, as we close this chapter, may I ask you:

Oral Roberts completed his mission!

Will you complete yours?

6

Philip the Evangelist

**"We . . . entered the house of Philip
the evangelist"** (Acts 21:8).

Books are important. Paul the Apostle must have thought
they were necessary:

> **"When you come, bring my coat that I left in
> Troas with Carpus; bring the books too"**
> (2 Timothy 3:18).

I hope that this book changes your life as one book did mine.
It was in 1977 that the Lord led me to a book (I trust He led you
to this one!). Just one chapter in that book helped give me the
clearest insight I had ever had as to who I am.

For years I had identified with the ministry of other
evangelists. As I read their biographies, I felt I could say, "I am
an evangelist." But what did that mean? I dreamed about doing
the same things that I had read evangelists did in the many
biographies that are, even as I type this, sitting behind me on

a bookshelf. Yet, for fifteen years, instead of evangelizing, I pastored churches.

I longed to be on the sawdust trail, but each time I tried (and I headed out the first time when I was twenty one years old), I would always come back, draped over the saddle! Why? There were various reasons. Sometimes because of finances, other times closed doors, often defeated by my struggles with sin. Then there was that depression that so often took the wind out of my sails. Yet, I can certainly attest to the truth:

> **"God never changes his mind when he gives gifts or when he calls someone"**
> (Romans 11:29 GW).

I could never get away for long from my call as a full-time evangelist. A defining moment of that calling happened when I was pastoring a church in Walla Walla, Washington. I had made it clear to my people that I felt I was an evangelist. After a service, my elder came to me and gave me something he thought I would find interesting.

He handed me a newsletter that he had received from Evangelist Kenneth Hagin. There was an article in it specifically about the ministry of an evangelist. In those few pages, Kenneth helped put all the loose pieces together of a fragmented idea of what I should be doing as an evangelist. It excited me and gave me hope. Maybe soon?

Before I share what Kenneth taught, I need to describe what happened soon after reading that newsletter. I was in a bookstore, looking among the titles, and I found one written by Donald Gee called *Now That You Have Been Baptized In The Spirit.* As I flipped through the pages, I saw where he was describing the office gift ministries. One chapter was devoted to the ministry of an evangelist.

Imagine my surprise when I discovered that Kenneth Hagin's article was almost a verbatim carbon copy of what Donald Gee wrote. Kenneth was accused of being a plagiarist. But I don't believe that. I have heard Kenneth preach too many times and heard him quote verse after verse or describe events down to the most minute detail, even the exact addresses of places he'd been in the past. Kenneth claimed that he had a photographic memory and could hear or read something once and after that quote it virtually verbatim.

Perhaps Kenneth had read the same book years previously or had heard Donald Gee preach on the subject. All I know is that the timing of this discovery and the duplication of teaching, to me, was but a second and sure witness from the Lord reinforcing other preachers' truth that became my truth.

Something I had somehow apparently missed in past readings of Acts, was what verse 21:8 said:

> **"On the next day we who were Paul's**
> **companions departed and came to Caesarea,**
> **and entered the house of Philip the evangelist,**
> **who was one of the seven, and stayed with him."**

Note three words,

"Philip the evangelist"

Philip is the only man in the Bible referred to as an "evangelist." Acts chapter 8 is devoted almost in its entirety to the ministry of Philip. In my book *Evangelist,* I referenced Philip's personal ministry to the Ethiopian Eunuch and how his wisdom in winning the Eunuch to Christ is a method we can all use in witnessing.

Four verses in the chapter tell us other interesting details of what this prototype evangelist did:

> **"Then Philip went down to the city of Samaria and preached Christ to them. And the multitudes with one accord heeded the things spoken by Philip, hearing and seeing the miracles which he did. For unclean spirits, crying with a loud voice, came out of many who were possessed; and many who were paralyzed and lame were healed. And there was great joy in that city"** (Acts 8:5-8).

If I am an evangelist, then shouldn't I also be ministering as Philip did? And what did he do?

Philip:

1. "went down to the city of Samaria"

An evangelist travels to cities and preaches. V. 40 adds that Philip:

> **"preached in all the cities till he came to Caesarea."**

Caesarea became his family's home base. Jesus, as the Great Evangelist, felt a similar call to various cities:

> **"And the crowd sought Him and came to Him, and tried to keep Him from leaving them; but He said to them, "I must preach the kingdom of God to the other cities also, because for this purpose I have been sent"** (Luke 4:42, 43).

Like Jesus, like Philip, evangelists have historically, with some exceptions, served in itinerant ministries. Then note that Philip:

2. "preached Christ to them"

A true evangelist, no matter what subject he happens to be preaching on, if sinners are present, will always want to preach the salvation message for at least a few minutes before giving an altar call. I have even preached an entire message to but two sinners in a church audience.

In fact, the desire of my heart is to not have to preach to saints at all but to preach all the time to crowds of sinners listening to the truth of the gospel. What further evidence would be needed to prove my call as an evangelist! And if I have the joy of preaching to crowds of sinners in the coming great revival, I will die satisfied!

3. "And the multitudes with one accord heeded the things spoken by Philip, hearing and seeing the miracles which he did."

The people responded to the gospel he preached. Why? Because not only were they hearing and seeing a preacher, but they were:

> **"hearing and seeing the MIRACLES which he did."**

I am convinced that God wants to perform miracles through evangelists and through you in these last days to reap the great final harvest of souls before Jesus returns (more about this in a later chapter).

4. "For unclean spirits, crying with a loud voice, came out of many who were possessed."

The casting out of a demon is a miracle that will often manifest as something that can be seen and heard (more about this also in a later chapter).

5. "and many who were paralyzed and lame were healed."

Thank God for gifts of healing when people feel the pain leave, a fever dissipates, or they start recovering after prayer. But miracles are far more dramatic. You can see and hear them. Imagine the sight in Samaria of someone who couldn't move one limb because of a stroke suddenly rising from a cot to run around and the sound of him shouting, "I'm healed! "I'm healed!" Or imagine someone who was lame, just as in Acts 3:7: "walking, and leaping, and praising God."

6. "And there was great joy in that city."

That is my goal, that when I leave a city a new joy remains there! I can still see the picture in my mind. I had just preached the last night of a revival in Wisconsin, had prayed for people, and was driving to a motel near the airport for an early morning flight. As I drove away, most people had stayed behind in the church. I could hear them singing and praising God joyfully. If I recall correctly, the pastor later reported that it went on for forty-five minutes or an hour.

People are depressed, sick, and broken. They need "great joy." We have their answer: the gospel of Christ, verified with miracles that can be seen and heard.

The things Philip did in Acts 8 are the things that I have been seeking to replicate since 1977. Philip was the prototype, the original model of the things evangelists should do. We can always improve upon a prototype, but we at least need to FIRST be doing the things which the prototype did! Those things are listed above.

In the following chapter, we'll learn that Philip had another title besides "Evangelist." These two titles clearly define the ministry of this office gift. Be sure as you read to continue to keep in mind what Paul wrote in 2 Tim. 4:5:

"do the work of an evangelist."

Meditate on these titles. . .

- **Philip the Evangelist**

- **Dea Warford the Evangelist**

- (Insert your name here) **the Evangelist**

7

DUNAMIS

"You're the God who makes things happen; you showed everyone what you can do"
(Psalm 77:14 MSG).

There are three types of people in the world:

- those who watch things happen,

- those who make things happen,

- and those who don't know anything is happening!

The above verse says God "makes things happen." If we understand how He does this, we can "perform miracles" too!

Reese Howells, the great intercessor, said,

> **"You may preach anything and everything without proving anything, which is nothing but spectacular theory! Faith must be substance before it becomes evidence!"**

"Substance," that's miracles seen and felt which become evidence!

Dynamite Power

It was 1981. My wife and I were living with my parents. I would evangelize as doors would open, and I would work jobs when I wasn't preaching. At the time, I had a part-time job soliciting for the Humane Society to check for up-to-date dog licenses.

I was preparing to head out the door when, while walking past my desk, I felt a sudden and unusual burden to pray.

I knelt at my office chair and almost immediately, the Lord whispered a word to my heart. It was,

"Power"

I knew it was real, and I knew the Lord wanted to reveal something of urgent importance to me. So, I didn't go to work that evening but instead got out my *Strong's Concordance* and made a word study of "power."

I discovered two Greek words translated "power" in the Authorized Version of the Bible. One is "exhousia," which means authority or the freedom to act. The other, and the word which hit me the hardest, is "dunamis."

Dunamis is the Greek word from which we get our English words dynamic, dynamo, and dynamite. Whereas exhousia means the freedom to act, dunamis means the ability and power to act.

In the authorized version dunamis has been translated into English not only as "power" and "miracles" but also as "mighty works" (Matthew 11:23), and "mighty deeds" (2 Corinthians 12:12).

What a personal revelation it was to me when I discovered that the word translated "miracles" not only refers to the power to do things but ALSO makes reference to the PERSON who does such things.

In Acts chapter 8, we saw that Philip worked miracles. This was because he walked in the office and anointing of an evangelist.

Philip The "Dunamis."

Ephesians 4:11 lists five office gifts,

> **"And He Himself gave some to be apostles, some prophets, some evangelists, and some pastors and teachers."**

Notice "evangelists" is one of the five gifts. In 1 Corinthians 12:28, Paul lists these offices again:

> **"And God has appointed these in the church: apostles second prophets, third teachers, after that miracles** (Greek: dunamis),**"**

Notice it doesn't mention pastors. Many believe the reason for this is because pastors ARE teachers, so they did not need to be included on this list. Pastoring, historically, is indeed a dual gift, shepherding and teaching sheep.

Then, you will notice that it doesn't mention evangelists. That is because, I am convinced, "miracles" ARE evangelists! Other translations evidence the concept that these are people who specialize in miracles: "those who do miracles" (NLT); "those who perform miracles" (GW).

V. 29 gives further confirmation of this:

> **"Are all apostles? Are all prophets? Are all teachers? Are all workers of miracles** (Greek: dunamis)**?"**

Why didn't Paul include the office of the evangelist in this list? I submit to you that this is because it was commonly understood in the New Testament church that the evangelist was a gift that would most closely be identified with miracles of healing.

Of course, throughout history some of the greatest miracle ministries were known as either apostles, prophets, or pastors.

We know historically and today that some have more dunamis than others, or at least have learned to tap into that resource in visible manifestations of power.

Jesus had this dunamis, loads of it! A woman said to herself:

> **"If only I may touch His clothes, I shall be made well** (and she was!)**."And Jesus immediately knowing Himself that power** (Greek: dunamis) **had gone out of Him, turned around in the crowd and said, "Who touched my clothes?"**

People made fun of Benny Hinn who, throwing his suit coat on someone in an audience, believed that there was an anointing of power on his coat to work miracles. This may be a highly debatable action, but it certainly isn't without scriptural precedent:

> "(Elisha) **took the mantle of Elijah that fell from him, and smote the waters, and said, Where** *is* **the LORD God of Elijah? and when he also had smitten the waters, they parted hither and thither: and Elisha went over"**
> (2 Kings 2:14 KJV).

Luke 1:17 speaks of:

> **"the spirit and power** (Greek: dunamis) **of Elijah."**

We know that Elisha received a double portion of Elijah's anointing (2 Kings 2). After Elisha died and was buried, even his bones still had dunamis left in them. Some men were fleeing an army and hurriedly dropped a corpse into Elisha's tomb. The dead man came back to life and walked again (2 Kings 13:21)!

Dunamis power can be transmitted by physical objects.

- In the Old Testament, the Urim and Thummim worn by the high priest could divine truth (Exodus 28:30).

- Naaman, the leper, was healed after dipping himself seven times in the River Jordan at the instruction of Elisha (2 Kings 5:14).

- A poultice of figs helped heal a dying king (2 Kings 20:7).

- The laying on of hands confers the power to heal sick bodies. (See Mark 16:17, 18, Acts 28:8, Luke 4:40, James 5:16).

- Anointing oil is one contribution to the healing ministry (See Mark 6:13, James 5:14).

- An angel stirred up a pool of water which resulted in miracles (John 5:4).

- And let's not forget Acts 19:11, 12

> **"Now God worked unusual miracles** (Greek: dunamis) **by the hands of Paul, so that even handkerchiefs or aprons were brought from his body to the sick, and the diseases left them and the evil spirits went out of them."**

It raises eyebrows when evangelists claim to have bottles of uniquely anointed oil, sell water from the Jordan River, or offer special prayer cloths. But Paul left the above example for them! Hey, that gives me an idea!!!

We know that ultimately it is the Holy Spirit that manifests the miracle, not people, not objects.

> **"...the power** (Greek: dunamis) **of the Lord was present to heal"** (Luke 5:17).

Let's be clear; DUNAMIS is the secret for any man or woman who would desire to work miracles or heal the sick.

In my studies of the lives of evangelists with healing ministries, with few exceptions, they each had to pay a great price to have such power. History proves it and my personal life illustrates it:

The more POWER you want, the greater price you will have to pay to obtain it. And then once you have the POWER, there is a price to pay to maintain the POWER.

While pastoring in Nampa, Idaho, in the late 1970s, I received a phone call from a newly graduated Rhema Bible College student (I'll refer to as Evangelist M.). Having the call of an evangelist on my life made me very predisposed to having guest evangelists in my pulpit, so I invited him to come to our church.

He was a good preacher and had an extraordinary "dunamis gift." When he prayed for people, they often received gold fillings in their teeth. The usual amalgam fillings would be replaced supernaturally by what appeared for sure to be pure gold! You can imagine what a scene this made in our little church.

M. would fast his breakfast, then I would pick him up for lunch daily. Then he wouldn't eat again until after the service. This morning fast was his apparent pattern when he was in a revival series.

Years later, I was pastoring, yet still longing to be on the evangelistic field. A preacher friend of mine in the district office said about evangelist M. "Now, M., he is an evangelist!" (Oh, and you mean I'm not?!?!" I thought it, but I didn't say it!)

Thank God the day came when I at last became reputed as "Evangelist" Dea Warford. In fact, one pastor said during one of my crusades in Reno, Nevada,

"Dea is the only true evangelist other than Mario Murillo that I have ever seen."

That pastor obviously hadn't met many of the true evangelists I have met! Still, to be mentioned in the same sentence with Mario Murillo was a real honor! Incidentally, Mario is my favorite evangelist (next to me, of course!).

Years later, I located the whereabouts of evangelist M. and had him speak at my church, where I was then pastoring in Hawaiian Gardens in Los Angeles County. M. was still a good preacher and he prayed for the sick and other things you would expect an evangelist to do. But,

No teeth were filled with gold!

After the meetings, I asked him why that was, and I'll never forget his answer:

"I know the price you have to pay to have a ministry like that."

He might as well have added:

"And I am just not willing to pay that price."

I don't know what price he felt he had to pay: long weeks away from home and family, fasting every day during revivals, pacing the floors in prayer all day long in his motel room, guarding his heart valiantly against carnality. . . or?

An evangelist who could have brought the Lord great glory through one of the rarest gifts of POWER among evangelists had instead settled for mediocrity. What a tragedy. May you and I pay the price for the POWER and keep paying the price so that at the end of our earthly journey, we don't have to admit,

"I just was not willing to pay the price"

DUNAMIS! It's your key, and the only key, to God's miracle power. Any Christian has the inner potential to work miracles as evangelists do,

"You shall receive power (Greek: dunamis)
when the Holy Spirit has come upon you"
(Acts 1:8).

If you are full of the Holy Spirit, then you already have dunamis working in you! If you are not, then do what Jesus told the disciples to do in Luke 24:49 NLT:

**"And now I will send the Holy Spirit, just as
my Father promised. But stay here in the city
until the Holy Spirit comes and fills you with
power** (Greek: dunamis) **from heaven"**
(Luke 24:49 NLT).

Stay in the city where God put you. Stay in the church where you are now. Stay in His presence. Stay in an expectant attitude of prayer. Stay, how long? Until:

**"the Holy Spirit comes and fills you with
DUNAMIS POWER"**

I had finished preaching and ministering around the altar at a church in the San Fernando Valley in Southern California. The pastor was with the treasurer counting my love offering for the evening. I was waiting impatiently to get my check, and head out for the long drive home, maybe with a stop for a shake on the way.

About everybody else had gone out. A woman, still lingering in the sanctuary, walked up to me and said she thought she might need deliverance. I began praying over her. I hadn't prayed long until she threw up on the church carpet. The vomit was an unusually bright orange color. Just about that time the pastor walked up to me, handed me the love offering check and said:

"When you come to a church, things happen!"

Apparently, he didn't like what "happened" to his church carpet, because no matter how many times I called him, he never invited me back again!

God grant that it will be said of you and every other last day Christian with the power of the Holy Spirit:

"When you come, things happen."

Don't just sit there watching things happen! Learn to partner with the Holy Spirit and be among those who have plugged into the resource of the dunamis and:

MAKE THINGS HAPPEN!

"You are the God who performs miracles" (Psalm 77:14 GW).

8

How to Heal the Sick

**"He sent them to preach the kingdom of
God and to heal the sick"**
(Luke 9:2).

While I was attending LIFE Bible College, I took some classes at nearby Azusa Pacific. While talking with the registrar about transferring some of my LIFE credits to get a degree through Azusa Pacific, he up front informed me that their college would not transfer units from the class of Divine Healing, which I had taken at LIFE. Many evangelicals, plain and simple, do not believe that Christians have a scriptural right to expect supernatural healing through prayer, as those of us from the traditional Pentecostal heritage do.

If you are not already aware of why praying for the sick is such a vital part of the history of the Pentecostal Movement, there are ample books in publication on the Pentecostal doctrine of what we call "Divine Healing" (in contradistinction to medical or natural healing). Thus, it is not necessary to have a comprehensive study of that subject in this book. If you want a more in-depth analysis on the matter of Divine Healing, I will refer you to three books at the end of this chapter.

One reason I wrote *Miracles Are Your Destiny* was to provide an all-in-one volume that would stand alone with the basics for any layperson who wants to be used of God in the last days. It is more a book of "how-to" than "why." It is less theoretical than it is practical. I hope you will keep this book ready at hand and refer to it often in the future, especially when the new anointing to heal begins to manifest.

There is no one specific "This is how you heal the sick" method to heal the sick. We know this by the many different healing methods Jesus used. However, after praying for the sick for over half of a century, I can vouch personally for the following approach to ministering healing to the sick. These enumerated steps will at least provide you with an elementary guide to assist you:

1. Become very familiar with biblical truths of Divine Healing.

Study the stories in the Gospels and Acts. Walk with Jesus and the Apostles through their healing experiences. Observe and learn from them. Memorize the great biblical healing promises. On the internet I found a list of fifty (https://www.biblestudytools.com/topical-verses/healing-bible-verses/). **Look** them up and print them.

2. Build your faith by meditating on and confessing healing texts.

The Bible reveals the necessity of faith to heal the sick.

"The prayer of faith (not "the prayer of

compassion" or "the prayer of sincerity") **will save the sick and the Lord shall raise him up"** (James 5:15).

Since faith is necessary to heal people, do you have enough faith personally to dare pray for the sick? And, if not, how can you obtain this essential faith?

"Faith comes by hearing and hearing by the word of God" (Romans 10:17).

Your faith to heal the sick will not come from this book, nor from stories you read of others who got results when they prayed for the sick. Books might encourage and inspire you. It is the Word alone that has the inherent power to increase your faith! Fill your heart and your mouth with it regularly!

The word is near you, even in your mouth and in your heart (that is, the Word of faith which we preach)" (Romans 10:8).

Notice faith is a "word." It is not an emotion or an idea. It is a word that comes from the mouth of God or your mouth!

3. Completely convince yourself that it is God's will to heal the sick through YOU.

You believe God can heal the sick, or you wouldn't be reading this book. Yet, it is NOT enough to think "God can heal the sick." Every Christian knows that! The question you must ask yourself is, "Will the Lord heal the sick through MY prayers." And you must answer yourself with a resounding, "Yes!" You know the answer is yes because of the clear testimony of the Word of God. Jesus taught us to pray:

"Thy kingdom come. Thy will be done in earth as it is in heaven" (Matt. 6:10 KJV).

There are no sick people in heaven. When we pray for the sick, we are endeavoring to see the kingdom of God established on earth. Healing is one of the benefits of being a part of His kingdom. Miracles of healing happened throughout the Old Testament through the ministry of prophets. The New Testament added many other classes of people to those who could be called "miracle workers":

- **Jesus healed the sick:** "Great multitudes (the Greek word means thousands) followed him and He healed them all" (Matthew 12:15).

- **The twelve disciples healed the sick:** "Then He called His twelve disciples together and gave them power . . . to cure diseases . . . He sent them to . . . heal the sick" (Luke 9:1, 2).

- **Seventy "others" healed the sick:** (aren't you an "other?"). "The Lord appointed seventy others also, and sent them two by two . . . He said to them. . .Heal the sick" (Luke 10:1, 2, 9).

- **Deacons healed the sick:** Acts 6:6 tells us that both Philip the evangelist and Stephen started out as deacons. Soon they were launched into healing ministries: "And Stephen, full of faith and power, did great wonders (Greek: dunamis) and signs among the people" (Acts 6:8).

- **Elders healed the sick:** "Is anyone among you sick? Let him call for the elders of the church, and let them pray over him" (James 5:14).

- A **"certain disciple named Ananias"** healed the sick: (see Acts 9:10-17). Are you a "disciple?"

- **Believers** (aren't you one of those guys?) **CAN heal the sick:** "These signs shall follow those who believe. . . they shall lay hands on the sick and they shall recover" (Mark 16:17, 18).

The Lord will use any available vessel to heal the sick. YOU be one of those vessels!

4. Determine a candidate to heal.

Ideally, you would be ministering at a pulpit in a church service and have plenty of time to teach Divine Healing to build faith in the congregants. Then you could offer to lay hands on those who believe to be healed and ask them to step forward to the altar. Unfortunately, if you are a layperson, you may never have this optimal scenario. But you don't need it!

The great Evangelist, John Wesley, said,

"The world is my pulpit."

Peter and John were walking into the Temple where a lame man was begging at the entrance. Peter took him by the hand and healed him. He didn't say, "Come on in and listen to me preach an hour, and then maybe the Lord will heal you." No, Peter believed God could heal anywhere and at any time. You believe the same.

The key is to be led by the Spirit, of course. That lame man had probably been begging at the Temple entrance many times. But on one very special day, Peter knew in his spirit that it was the man's time to be healed. You will pass by many people who are hobbling along, some with a cane or crutches, and some being pushed in a wheelchair. Is it this one or that one's time?

Peter had prepared himself for that miracle moment. You must prepare yourself for your miracle moments which are waiting just ahead for you. In a later chapter, we will discuss how to be ready to be used as an instrument of healing and all other supernatural gifts of the Spirit.

5. Discern if the person you want to pray for is ready.

Not everybody is ready to be healed:

> **"Jesus saw the man lying there and knew that he had been sick for a long time. So Jesus asked the man, "Would you like to get well?"** (John 5:6 GW).

A man came forward after one of my altar calls walking with a cane. I assumed he wanted to be healed and started to pray for his healing when he whispered in my ear, "I get paid by social security for this!" He wanted God to bless him, but not by healing him and making him go back to work!

Others would like to be healed, but just do not have faith for their healing. Even Jesus needed people to have faith to receive a miracle:

> **"Now He could do no mighty work** (Greek: dunamis) **there, except that He laid His hands on a few sick people and healed them. And He marveled because of their unbelief"** (Mark 6:5).

If Jesus was limited in what He could do because of people's unbelief, how much more are you and I limited by unbelief?

I have been at churches where I have watched as people cautiously walked into the sanctuary with a cane. My heart has leaped with hope and faith that they might be healed that morning. I have announced that we would be praying for the sick after I preached. But, oh so often, around noon, before we could pray for them, I sadly watched as they left the church to go out for their lunch.

There is so much unbelief in our nation today. I attended a healing crusade at the Pond soccer stadium in Anaheim, California. Benny Hinn was ministering that day to thousands. There was a long row between sections where quite a few sat in wheelchairs, some with special breathing assisting devices or other severe handicaps and health issues. To my knowledge, not one of them was healed during that service.

Now, this is not to disparage Benny Hinn's ministry. During the same service, I heard actor Pat Boone's wife, Shirley, testify of being healed of Lupus. I later read that she went home and said to Pat, "Watch this!" With that, she began running up the stairs, something she apparently had not been able to do for some time.

A long line of unhealed, desperately sick souls is a sobering commentary on how rare it is (at least now!) to see extraordinary miracles of healing in America, even by those reputed to have a powerful gift. On the other hand, there are great evangelistic crusades in places like Africa, where we read of amazing miracles happening commonly.

So, if Jesus couldn't see great miracles in a city that might have been the equivalent of New York; if Benny Hinn couldn't see great miracles in Los Angeles; then, if you or I will ever see great miracles, we may just have to wait expectantly for the coming mantle of faith and power to fall on our nation. And, once it does, we must be ready to do as Paul did,

> **"And in Lystra a certain man without strength in his feet was sitting, a cripple from his mother's womb, who had never walked. This man heard Paul speaking. Paul, observing him intently and seeing that he had faith to be healed, said with a loud voice, 'Stand up straight on your feet!' And he leaped and walked"** (Acts 14:8-10).

"Seeing" in your spirit that certain sick folks have "faith to be healed" will result in miracles!

Important: never push people beyond their faith! I have pushed sinners into praying a sinner's prayer who were not at all ready to make that commitment, but just couldn't say no to a salesman.

I have had women come up to me in the altar area after giving an invitation for those who need healing to come forward. They've said, "That's my husband sitting on the back row. He needs healing. Could you please come and pray for him." I wouldn't do it! If they don't have enough faith to walk forward fifty feet to give God at least a chance to heal them, then I figure I don't have the faith to make up for their unbelief!

When you feel ready to pray for someone's healing and discern that they are ready also, I suggest you do the following.

6. Briefly help them to prepare to receive their healing.

Quote a few Scriptures to refresh their memory of their right to expect God to answer prayer. I have often quoted two:

> **"The things that are impossible with men** (they likely have had doctors fail them) **are possible with God"** (Luke 18:27).

> **"If two of you agree on earth concerning anything that they ask, it will be done for them by My Father in heaven"** (Matthew 18:19).

By doing this, you have, in essence, preached a mini-sermon on divine healing, like a healing crusade evangelist!

7. Invite others, if available, to join you by laying their hands on the sick along with yours.

This accomplishes several important things. It helps take attention off you while helping the church realize that their prayers are important too! Women can lay their hands on the more private parts of a women's body (hips, lower backs, stomachs, etc.). Men can do the same with men.

When several pray and a person receives healing, the glory goes more to Jesus (instead of one person). In all fairness, it likely will be another person's faith or their anointing that tips the scales anyway! Those who may have seen the first healing in answer to their prayers will have been greatly encouraged!

8. Lay hands on their sick body, as near the area of pain or disease as modesty allows.

There must be a reason that Jesus said in Mark 16:18,

> **"They shall lay <u>HANDS</u> on the sick."**

The power of God is usually transmitted through a believer's hands. If you are filled with the Holy Spirit, you have the dunamis in you, remember? Let it seep, or a better word "flow," out of your hands into some sick body!

9. PRAY!

Pray out loud. Only one place in the Bible did anyone pray silently (1 Samuel 1:3). Even then, Hannah at least moved her lips when she prayed. Remember, "faith comes by HEARING." Let the sick person and everyone nearby hear your faith-filled bold words!

Resist thoughts of doubt or unworthiness hindering your faith. It is called in James 5:15:

"The prayer of faith."

The act of praying for the sick, in itself, shows a measure of faith. Speak healing promises over sick bodies. Doubts will surely come but cast them down (2 Corinthians 10:3-5). Make an unwavering decision to stand boldly on the authority of the Word of God and the Name of Jesus!

Unbelief is a choice! Thomas chose to not believe in John 20:25:

"Unless I see. . .I WILL NOT believe"

Faith also is a choice:

> **"he who does not believe God has made**
> **Him a liar, because he has not believed the**
> **testimony that God has given of His Son."**

In John 17:17, Jesus believed God wouldn't lie and thus said,

"Your word is truth."

Choose to believe the truth of God's Word concerning Divine Healing. Jesus' testimony in 4:18 was,

"He has sent Me to heal."

Make that your same testimony! Tell yourself (and the devil), "He has sent me to heal!"

10. Expect a miracle.

You are in anticipation of a miracle. Give the Lord every opportunity to perform one! Immediately after prayer, ask the person if they can tell a difference.

If they were in pain, ask, "What percentage of the pain is gone?" If they couldn't lift their arm, encourage them to lift it as high as they can. If they couldn't walk without pain, encourage them to walk about some.

Experience shows that, for whatever reasons, it often takes a few minutes to begin seeing results. If there is some improvement, pray again. Jesus prayed for a blind man who received partial healing and then prayed for him a second time (See Mark 8:24). Elijah prayed for a dead boy three times (1 Kings 17:21). I have prayed for many people several times until we had significant improvement or complete healing. Let your faith and the Spirit guide you.

11. What to do when they are not healed.

First: Make sure they do not have unforgiveness toward anyone. Time and again, someone in my prayer line couldn't get healed until they were willing to forgive someone.

I was ministering at a church in Illinois. A middle-aged man came for prayer and said he was suffering from back pain. We prayed, but he wasn't healed. I then asked him if he had unforgiveness toward anyone. He did and told the story of how he was a pastor until someone sexually molested his daughter. He was so filled with anger and hatred that he left the ministry and became a truck driver. One day a chain securing a load snapped and swung around, hitting him in the back. He had significant back problems ever since.

When I explained to him that his unforgiveness was hindering his healing and why he had to forgive the man, he became convinced. He chose to forgive the man and did so right on the platform. We then prayed again, and the pain left, and he was able to bend over and touch his toes for all to see, something he couldn't do for a long time.

Either before you even start praying or at least, after you do, but don't get results, say to them:

"Sometimes if we have unforgiveness in our hearts, that hinders receiving healing. Can you think of anybody from your past or present you are harboring anger, hatred, or unforgiveness toward?"

If they say they do, encourage them to forgive and after they do, pray again.

Second: Consider the possibility that you are dealing with a "spirit of infirmity" we read about in Luke 13:11-13, 16:

> **"And behold, there was a woman who had**
> **a SPIRIT OF INFIRMITY eighteen years,**
> **and was bent over and could in no way raise**
> **herself up. But when Jesus saw her, He called**

her to Him and said to her, "Woman, you are loosed from your infirmity." And He laid His hands on her, and immediately she was made straight, and glorified God."

Here is a revelatory testimony concerning this subject:

"For forty years, I had Gran Mal seizures, about every other day, really bad. I have scars and bruises from falling down. I had to spend time in hospitals. I am fifty-six-years-old now. I took 100 mg of Phenobarbital five times a day since I was eleven and 100 mg of Dilantin five times a day. I had a speech problem as a child. I couldn't go to school, as I was handicapped. I couldn't hold jobs because once they found out about my condition, they would fire me. The night Dea prayed, when you were at our church about four years ago, DEMONS WERE MANIFESTING. I broke my glasses. I hit you. But, since the day you prayed for me, I haven't had one seizure. I can work now. I am a teacher. I tried to find help. I went to priests and other evangelists. I kept searching, but they couldn't help me."

Nikki Ploski,
Palm Desert, California

"So ought not this woman, being a daughter of Abraham, whom Satan has bound — think of it--for eighteen years, be loosed from this bond on the Sabbath?" (Luke 13:16).

I think we can say, as Jesus said of a woman bound by Satan for 18 years:

"Shouldn't a woman whom Satan had bound for 40 years (in the above testimony), **be loosed?"**

I believe Nikki had a "spirit of infirmity." Apparently, the "priests and other evangelists" who "couldn't help" her did not understand, where there are physical infirmities, it is not always enough to pray, "Oh, Lord, please heal them!" NO, a demon may need to be cast out! (We will have much more to say about demons and how to cast them out in Part Two of this book).

This is not some strange, personal doctrine I'm teaching. Historically, Pentecostals have believed that all sickness is caused by Satan: indirectly through the fall of man, as the result of sin, or directly by demonic power.

If the sickness is a result of the fall, a medical doctor might be able to help. If the sickness is a result of sin, repentance could help. If it is a demon, cast it out!

If you have prayed for someone and feel you have done all you can do for the time being, encourage them to keep believing and to fight the "good fight of faith." If they seem downcast because of no apparent improvement, remind them that Mark 16:18 says,

"They shall recover."

Recovery can take time. Also, James 5:16 says,

"The Lord will raise him up."

It doesn't add "within seconds." Many healings are gradual. Leave them with the hope of that. Then, you believe that your prayer "launched" the healing process. Before I pray for the sick, I will often prepare the people by saying something like,

"Some are healed instantly. Others receive partial healing. Or you might sense no change at this time. We have received testimonies of people who go home and a few hours later have more relief or even wake up in the morning pain-free. Let's pray for an instant miracle but thank God for any healing touch that begins today."

Why some are healed, and others aren't is the mystery of the ages and can be baffling for miracle workers. Yet, there are often explainable reasons why we don't see more consistency in divine healing. That isn't the scope of this chapter, but you may find helpful information in the books listed below.

Here is your homework for today, student of the Word:

1. Start practicing the above in your home church and watch and pray for healing opportunities outside the church among friends, neighbors or even strangers.

2. Prepare a prominent place on your bookshelf to keep this "How to book" after you are finished reading it. Make it ready at hand for when the next Healing Revival fires begin to fall!

3. Order one or more of the books listed if you are hungry to be used of God to heal the sick and I have but whetted your appetite. They are all available at Amazon.com:

HEALING THE SICK by T.L. Osborn, Harrison House, Tulsa, Oklahoma, 1952, 2003. . .

. . . is considered a classic. It was the book I read when I launched into my first evangelistic outreaches in 1973, and it helped inspire me in praying for the sick. Evangelist Osborn was no theorist; he healed the sick, including blind eyes and deaf ears, in over 70 countries during his ministry. I highly recommend it!

CHRIST THE HEALER by F.F. Bosworth, Chosen, Grand Rapids, 1924, 1948. . .

. . .predates T.L. Osborn's book. It helped fan the flames of divine healing during the Healing Revival. It is also considered a classic and is a must for your library if you need more inspiration and would like to explore the doctrinal foundation of the Healing Revival.

THE ESSENTIAL GUIDE TO HEALING by Bill Johnson, Chosen, Minneapolis, Minnesota, 2011. . .

. . .is a more recent publication. Bethel Church in Redding, California, where Bill Johnson pastors, is a healing center where people come in from worldwide. Healing Evangelist Randy Clark, who also has a renowned healing ministry, co-wrote the book.

These are but three books of many. Whatever books you choose for further study, you will be doing so in obedience to the scriptural command:

> **"Study to shew thyself approved unto God, a workman** (miracle worker!) **that needeth not to be ashamed, rightly dividing the word of truth"** (2 Timothy 2:15 KJV).

PART TWO

CASTING OUT DEMONS

"I came from a very ungodly home. God had given me a vision that was filled with His joy. But, when I tried to use that vision, all I could see were demons. Also, I could not feel the joy He had promised me. I explained this to Dea. He started praying and taking authority over the demon. I got this horrible tearing pain in my heart, and then I could tell it had left. The joy came flooding in and also an unasked-for peace filled me. The next day, I could feel incredible joy and peace. The vision is sketchy, but now I see things of God, not the ugly demons Satan had tormenting me. Three weeks later, it is like there is a whole new realm that has opened for God to work in me and clean me up, big time. That night was like the door God opened."

Lisa
Missoula, Montana

9

A Strange Ministry

"John's clothes were woven from coarse camel hair. . . For food he ate locusts and wild honey"
(Matthew 3:4 NLT).

John the Baptist was a strange man! It was prophesied over me when I was a young man that God had called me to "a strange ministry." There is nothing on earth stranger than casting out demons. People screaming, spitting, vomiting, shaking violently, or making a face at you like some monster is strange indeed. Yet, I have had all those things and more happen while casting out demons. I had a long journey and a steep learning curve to climb for God to use me in this ministry.

> **"John said to Jesus, "Teacher, we saw someone forcing demons out of a person by using the power and authority of your name. We tried to stop him because he was not one of us. Jesus said, "Don't stop him! No one who works a _miracle_ in my name can turn around and speak evil of me"** (Mark 9:38, 39 GW).

The disciples reported to Jesus that there was a man "forcing demons out." Jesus then described that work as a "miracle" (highlighted and underscored above). God called me to a miracle ministry. Thus, if casting out a demon is a miracle then you would expect the Lord to train me in casting out demons wouldn't you? And train me He did!

My Strange Journey

I was a minister of youth at the Upland, California Foursquare church. It was about 1970. On a Christian radio station, I heard the announcement of a Tent Crusade in the Riverside area. My sister, Elaine, and I decided to go. As we drove along the highway looking for the tent, we couldn't find it. Then, on a piece of cardboard, we saw the word "Tent" with an arrow. Laughing, we turned down a dirt road until we came upon the tent, set up in an empty field.

The speaker that night was one "Sister Gladys," a middle-aged woman who had been a missionary to Africa. She was a powerful preacher and told some dramatic stories of her experiences in Kenya. I was impressed and took some of my youth with me to hear Sister Gladys.

I don't remember anything else that happened except one quite amazing thing. While just sitting on a folding chair in the audience, a teenage girl in our youth group received the Holy Spirit. She began speaking out loud in tongues without anybody laying hands on her, something I didn't remember ever seeing before.

We began to spend time with Sister Gladys to get to know her better. Before long, my sister was a member of Sister Gladys' small Church in Covina. It was called "The Garden of Prayer."

And it fit the name! There were all-night prayer meetings every Saturday. Sister Gladys knew how to pray! I suppose she had to learn how to pray as a primitive missionary in the jungles of Africa!

One Saturday night, I kind of "backslid" for the night and went to the drive-in to see a "forbidden" R-rated movie. Afterward, I felt guilty about it but decided to drive over to Sister Gladys' all-night prayer service.

That night a woman named Wanda sang a lovely Christian song. Before long, however, that same woman fell to the floor, manifesting demons. Some of the ladies held her down while Sister Gladys led the charge, kneeling over her doing spiritual warfare. Later, it was revealed that Wanda slept around with men. She even had an affair with one of the guest speakers at The Garden of Prayer.

Demonic manifestations may have been common in Kenya, but Covina? We observed this bizarre scene unfolding before our eyes in the Garden of Prayer, probably a first for most of us. Sister Gladys took control of the situation and leaned over Wanda, speaking to the demons, commanding them to go.

I sat, nervous as a cat in a rocking chair factory, waiting in anticipation for the demons in Wanda to turn her head toward me, point her finger, and say, "We know what you did tonight!" Thankfully, that didn't happen. But I had experienced my first up-close deliverance session and escaped with my sin still hidden, though not from the Lord!

Don't Blame Demons for Everything!

In the summer of 1974, I attended the Church on the Way in Van Nuys, California. I was also on the maintenance staff, and my wife and I lived in one of the church-owned apartments. I was struggling in my marriage and with sin and was counseling with Pastor Hayford about it. He referred me to a staff member for further counseling.

After telling her of my problems, she said, "It's a demon. Fast three days, and then we will cast it out." I began fasting but was troubled about all this and asked the Lord to speak to me out of the Word. I opened my Bible to 2 Cor. 7:1:

> **"Therefore, having these promises, beloved, let us cleanse ourselves from all filthiness of the flesh and spirit, perfecting holiness in the fear of God."**

The phrase "let us cleanse ourselves" hit me hard. I knew Dea Warford. I was a stubborn, disobedient Christian. What good would it do to cast out a "spirit" as long as I was walking in the "filthiness of the flesh." I knew God was calling me to deal with my sin, and I was to do so through "these promises" (in the Word of God). I knew what the Word said about sin and how to overcome it. I couldn't blame my willful sin on someone else, even a demon! I didn't go through with that deliverance session with the church counselor.

Shortly after that, I was walking down the hall and noticed that counselor with several other staff members ministering deliverance to another staff member in the kitchen area. When she saw me, I overheard her tell the others"

"Don't let Dea in here!"

She might as well have added, "These demons might jump over into Dea, or worse, his demons might jump on some of us!" I was a minister of the gospel and a Bible College graduate, yet I was unworthy even to help them pray. Humiliated and embarrassed, I headed away from them (where I belonged!).

Years later, that same young man, unworthy to pray against evil spirits, has the joy of casting out demons around this nation. It's ironic. But it also says this: "If God can use someone kicked out of a church kitchen, then God can use you, a fellow sinner saved by grace! "

God hadn't taken off my training wheels yet. In 1977, I began making some serious decisions to walk in holiness before the Lord. I was pastoring a church in Walla Walla, Washington. It was here that I was to learn about the deliverance ministry.

During a district conference, I was visiting over dessert with a couple of other pastors. One of them, Rev. Phillips, had been my professor at LIFE Bible College. We began to talk about demonic possession, and Rev. Phillips said, "To say that a Christian could be demon-possessed is blasphemy."

I remember being troubled about the conversation. Later that evening, I asked the Lord, "Can a Christian be demon-possessed?" I then opened my Bible to Ps. 32:8:

> **"I will instruct you and teach you in the way**
> **you should go: I will guide you with my eye."**

With that promise, I trusted the Lord to teach me the truth about the subject. And teach me he did! How? He led me to a book to "instruct" me and "teach" me.

The Book

Back in Walla Walla, He "guide(d) me with His eye." While perusing a bookshelf in a store, I found a book, written by Don

Basham, called *Can a Christian Have a Demon?* I excitedly bought it and could hardly wait to read it.

Don Basham was one of the leaders of the Charismatic Renewal. During the Charismatic movement, casting out demons, which was previously mainly relegated to back-alley small Pentecostal churches, was by the 1970s actively performed in mainline churches. Catholic, Episcopalian, Methodist, Presbyterian, and others were getting in on the action.

Then there was our little Walla Walla Bible Center. The weirdest people were coming to our services! The local college flasher attended our Church! They were looking for him, and he was one of my "members!" A bisexual man would come to services swinging a woman's purse as high as he could. We had neurotics. We may have had psychotics!

My elder, Jim Rowan, married with an infant daughter, came to me one day and said, "Pastor Dea, I know we want our church to grow. . .but the KIND of people who are coming to our church!" I didn't know how to respond, but I had to agree with him. This wasn't what I wanted to be when I grew up!

Can a Christian Have a Demon convinced me that many of the problems in the lives of the people attending my Church were demonic in origin. Thus, I began fasting and praying every Thursday. I would head for the Church, kneel in the sanctuary, and ask God to give me a deliverance ministry to set the captives free.

I didn't have to wait long before my long ago prophesied "strange ministry" events began to happen.

10

I Meet Demons

**"A man with an unclean spirit . . . had his
dwelling among the tombs"**
(Mark 5:2, 3).

Among the Tombs

A man in the Walla Walla church, we'll call "Ed," asked to borrow $20.00. He said he had a job now at the cemetery (that should have told me something!) and promised to pay me when he got his first check on Friday. When Friday came, I called and asked him if he could now pay me back. Ed said, "I received my paycheck, but I took it to the bank, and it bounced!" I told him, "They can't do that! Let's go down to the cemetery right now." I drove to his apartment, and he joined me in my car.

When we arrived at the cemetery, I saw several men working. I walked over to them with Ed tagging along, introduced myself, and explained, "This man worked here this past week, got his paycheck and when he tried to cash it at the bank, it bounced." The men smiled and looked at me incredulously. Ed turned immediately to walk away saying out loud, "Yes, I worked here and got a check and it bounced." Embarrassed, I excused myself and joined Ed now sitting in my car.

As we pulled away, I said, "Come on, Ed. I'm your pastor. Tell me the truth. You really didn't work here, did you?" He shot back, "Yes, I did, I did work here." Something came over me and I said, "You're lying to me!" He retorted, "Nobody's going to call me a liar!" When we stopped, he jumped out of the car.

I drove along beside him and pleaded with him to get back into the car, apologizing. But he was mad and cried, "No!" Well then I was mad! I parked the car and started heading towards him. When I headed towards him, he took off running. When he took off running, I started running after him.

Here was the pastor of the Walla Walla Bible Center, chasing his member down the street passing house after house, running as fast as I could. He was younger and faster than I was, and I couldn't catch him. Soon I stopped. Huffing and puffing, I shook my fist towards those invisible beings that I felt had him bound and cried to the top of my voice:

"You foul devil. I'll learn to cast you out, no matter what it takes!"

Discouraged and feeling powerless, I walked back to the car, wholly defeated. I moped around the house feeling depressed and sorry for myself. The irony of this event centered around a cemetery, "among the tombs," didn't hit me until this writing.

My First Deliverance Session

That same afternoon, I received a phone call. It was from a woman I had never met who asked if she could counsel with me. I invited her to come to my office in my home, which she did that afternoon.

As she sat across from my desk, she described a sordid tale, a tale like I had never heard before. She would feel something reach out and touch her in the night. Her five-year-old daughter would wake up screaming. I listened as she told her story, then asked, "What do you feel when I say, 'the Blood of Jesus?'" She said, "I feel angry!" I casually explained, "It's a demon, and I'm going to cast it out (as if I had been doing it all my life!)."

When I walked around the desk to lay hands on her, she grabbed my long shirt sleeves and began to wrestle with me around the office (And I have been wrestling with demons ever since!). I didn't know what I was doing, so I just began to do the things I had read. It took a few weeks for my wife and me to meet and pray with her further. Finally, during a midweek service, she raised her hand while seated with the congregation. I acknowledged her. With a smile, she said,

"I'm free!"

I had entered into a new dimension of life-changing ministry.

A book taught me how to cast out demons. This book will teach you also. Don't stop reading now!

From time to time, over the next several years, I would have more "strange ministry" experiences. Let me share several:

A Prostitute is Delivered

In the late '70s' I pastored a church in Nampa, Idaho. My wife and I had a particular Sunday night routine. After the evening services, she would fix tacos (Now, for you who live further up north or back east, a taco is made of a thin corn shell, filled with meat, cheese, lettuce, and...oh, never mind!).

As we enjoyed our tacos, we would watch the NBC *Sunday Mystery Movie.* Older people will remember them: one week *McCloud,* the next *McMillan and Wife,* and then *Columbo,* my favorite! My son Nathan bought me the whole *Columbo* series on DVD's, and I enjoy watching them by myself, especially when I travel (neither my wife nor son like *Columbo!*).

After one service, I was anxious to finish shaking hands and greeting people after preaching a long sermon (my family always got on to me for preaching so long. They had no appreciation for the importance of the things I had to say!). As I was about to join my wife for tacos next door, suddenly and unexpectedly, I had a burden to pray. It was so extraordinary, I felt I had to respond to the prompting. I told Kathy to go on to the parsonage, a part of the old church structure (which I heard had at one time been a slaughter house!), just across a hallway.

Then I began to wage spiritual warfare. I paced about the church, praying, speaking in tongues, praising, rebuking the devil, and anything I could think of to do. After a while, the burden lifted off me. It was too late to join Kathy in watching the movie, so I went to my office to study.

The phone rang. It was Rick Mansfield, my assistant pastor. He had to report something quite urgent to me. He had been called over to the home of a young married couple in our church whom I'll refer to as Tim and Ann.

After the couple had returned home from the service, something happened. Tim needed help. I had no idea about this, but Ann had previously been a prostitute. As she was talking to her husband, suddenly she told him, "I'm going back to the streets." He asked, "Why?" She said, "Because you don't satisfy me as they did. You don't beat me!"

My assistant would later report that when he got to the house, she was holding a knife and said, "We're going to kill her!" ("We're," plural!). Rick said he thought she was acting, until she fell against the side of the doorjamb so hard that he, "knew she wouldn't do that if she were faking it."

By the time I arrived at their home, Ann had calmed down some. When they told me everything that had happened, I knew she needed deliverance and we began to cast out the demons. After a while, she sat up, looked at her husband and asked, "Are they gone?" And yes, I believe they were! Hallelujah! She didn't go back to the streets, and that was the last time we were called to her house because of demons!

Notice the pattern that night:

1. God gave me a burden to pray.

2. I waged spiritual warfare, instead of eating and watching television.

3. A previously hidden demon manifested. We confronted it and a deliverance resulted.

This is a pattern you need to expect in your life. But consider this: what if I hadn't obeyed the Holy Spirit's call to warfare? What if I had just thought, "Oh, I'll pray later" or "I'm hungry and deserve some R & R?"

Somebody has to pay the price to bring deliverance to tormented souls. Do you feel a burden rising within you even as you read this book? Is God calling you to cast out demons? Keep reading!

Knocking on Tombstones

During that same period, while pastoring in Nampa, a visitor came to our church service. My assistant Rick quietly reported to me, "That man has a spirit of lust." God used Rick in the gifts of the Spirit, and I assumed he knew this by the Spirit. After the service, I told the man, "Do you need deliverance from anything. I'd like to help." He admitted he did and followed me into my office.

After asking him some of the basic questions that I ask those seeking deliverance, he told me quite a story. He had been involved in witchcraft. He said he would go out to the cemetery and knock on the tombstones to communicate with the dead (there are those tombs again!). He also, in satanic rituals, would drink blood.

After I led him in a prayer of renunciation of the occult, I began taking authority over spirits of witchcraft. He soon began to cough, which is not unusual at all for those with demons. Then the cough turned into the sound one makes when gagging and about to throw up. I had read about this kind of thing, so I grabbed an empty quart jar that I happened to have in my office.

He spat up something into the jar. It didn't look like saliva, and it didn't look like vomit. It was some disgusting mucous-like substance. He gagged up until the jar was maybe 1/8th full. Next, he began laughing. It was loud and weird, like some witch's laugh from a horror movie. After a season of warfare, both he and I were satisfied that he had experienced a real deliverance. The next time I saw him, he said,

"I didn't know you could be this happy being a Christian.'

My brother, my sister, there are many Christians out there who are very unhappy. It's the work of hell in their lives. We can set them free!

A Monster

In August of 1980, I was preaching in a church in the San Bernardino area of California. When I called people forward for prayer, a young man we'll call "Bob," maybe 20 years old, came forward. After laying hands on him to pray, he began jerking around and fell to the floor. It was apparent to me that it was a demonic manifestation.

I loudly commanded a demon to leave. After a few minutes, Bob rose to his feet, smiling, and sat back down. People were rejoicing. They had seen a miracle! However, I knew in my spirit that he wasn't completely free yet.

After the service, I asked the pastor if I could use his church office to counsel and pray further with Bob. He was happy to let me. While we sat on a sofa, I began asking Bob questions. I discovered that he had been involved in witchcraft. So had his father, which explained why he had bolted out of the sanctuary and out the back door in the middle of my sermon. I have had more than one through the years do the same. Demons want to get away from anyone that they know could cast them out!

I had Bob renounce his involvement in the occult and then began boldly taking authority over any demons. He grabbed a couple of pillows from the sofa and started shaking them over his head as he sneered, crying loudly, "Ugh! Ugh! Ugh!"

The pastor opened the door, peeked in, saw what was going on, and shut the door! I couldn't believe it! He left me alone in there to deal with those demons while he was safely outside!

Bob cowered in the corner awhile and then abruptly turned toward me. He had bitten himself by now and, with blood dripping down his chin, slowly headed towards me with his hands extending like claws. His face was distorted and smiling like some monster delighted to eat you (I see where Hollywood gets its inspiration for horror movies!).

I was wondering if I shouldn't crawl out a window to escape! But I believed I had authority over demons as the Word promised, so determined to continue in the fight.

I had read about how demonized people will try to choke you. Sure enough, his claws slowly headed towards my throat. At first, I did the natural thing and lifted my hands to protect myself. But then, the Holy Spirit quickened a verse to my heart,

> **"Behold, I give unto you power to tread upon serpents and scorpions, and over all the power of the enemy: and nothing shall by any means hurt you"** (Luke 10:19).

With that promise, I took one of the greatest steps of faith I had ever taken in my life. I dropped my hands to my side and said:

"In the name of Jesus!"

Oh, the power in that Name! I wish you could have seen it! It was as though an invisible hand pushed Bob back against the wall away from me. I followed him around the room, continued praying and commanding demons until, at last, back on the sofa, with his hands raised toward the ceiling, he screamed as the demons came out!

A few months later, I heard from the pastor that Bob was attending the church with his girlfriend, apparently moving on with God!

I have not exaggerated these stories. I am an eyewitness to the reality of hellish beings making people miserable. Perhaps you know someone "living among the tombs" (metaphorically speaking). I am a witness that demons are "touching people in the night," binding souls in prostitution and other sexual perversions, even driving some to a fascination with the dead, or making them like a monster!

These are my true stories.

I am an exorcist.

I cast out demons!

Won't you too become an exorcist?

11

Christians And Demons?

**"But Paul, greatly annoyed, turned and said
to the spirit, "I command you in the name of
Jesus Christ to come out of her." And he came
out that very hour"** (Acts 16:18).

Notice that Paul told a demon to "come out." You can't
"come out" of a place that you are not "in." The Word, when
referring to demons, never says "cast away." Time and again
the specific phrase, "cast out" is used, or as Paul did, when
speaking to a demon, commanded it to:

"come out."

The significance of this, to you and me, is that the Bible way
to get rid of demons is ALWAYS to make them "come out" from
wherever they may be hiding. Most Christians wouldn't have
a problem with this analysis. The problem, however, is if we
suggest that there are Christians that have a demon "in" them
and thus we have to "cast out" that demon. A DEMON. . .IN
A CHRISTIAN? (Don't turn that dial. . .I mean, don't click that
remote control!). Dare to read on!

A Pastor's Wife

"My name is S.J. My husband is Pastor of the . . . Christian Center. . .Wyoming. Dea was evangelizing at a Foursquare Church. The evening I was there, he shared on spiritual warfare and deliverance. As the evening went on, I became sick to my stomach and was shaking. Dea called those of us up who needed healing from childhood trauma. I had been sexually abused as a child. He began to cast out demons of torment, guilt, shame, fear, hatred, and anger. I began writhing, shaking, choking, and gagging. How far out of control I felt. I felt like I couldn't breathe, like I was suffocating. I remember spitting up and crying. Boy, do those demons hold on! Praise God I have been set free. What awesome spiritual darkness has left me, and the Glory of God is shining through! I have been delivered. Thank you, God."

What you just read was a testimony from a pastor's wife. Think about that for a moment, especially if you are convinced, as many Christians are, that a Christian cannot have a demon. I believed the same way at one time and felt that there were scriptures to prove that.

The Bible does NOT clearly say one way or the other: "a Christian can have a demon" or "a Christian cannot have a demon." Yet there are several verses that, at first glance, might seem to indicate that a Christian cannot have a demon. These same verses have been used repeatedly to defend that doctrine. Let's examine a few of those "proof texts":

> **"You are of God, little children, and have overcome them, because He who is in you is greater than he who is in the world"** (1 John 4:4).

Isn't this verse saying that Jesus is in a Christian and Satan is in the world, thus proving a Christian can't have a demon? No, it doesn't say that! "He who is in the world" is written in the context of the previous verse (3),

> **"And this is the spirit of the Antichrist, which you have heard was coming, and is now already in the world."**

Christians don't have the Antichrist spirit in them! We are not under that influence. This "Antichrist spirit" is not just one lowly demon. This "spirit" refers to the ongoing widespread control that Satan has on earth, which will increase more and more until THE Antichrist appears.

> **"We know that we are children of God and that the world around us is under the control of the evil one"** (1 John 5:19 NLT).

This control over the world does not, however, indicate that Christians are completely exempt from any "control of the evil one." The verse before says,

> **"We know that whoever is born of God does not sin; but he who has been born of God keeps himself, and the wicked one does not touch him"** (1 John 5:18).

Verse 18 is one of those many promises that must be actuated by faith and obedience. Sincere Christians come into my prayer lines all the time who love Jesus and hate their sin, but they still have struggled with sin for years. Because they are "born of God," through His grace and power, they "keep themselves" from allowing the devil to "touch" them.

This word "touch" ("Hapto" in the original Greek) is the same word used in 1 Corinthians 7:1,

> **"It is good for a man not to touch** (Hapto) **a woman."**

Just as a man can touch a woman and go too far until it ends up in adultery (with perhaps an unwanted child forming inside!), so a Christian must "keep himself" from permitting the devil's touch to lead him into greater sin and bondage and unwelcomed beings forming inside.

1 John 5:18 couldn't possibly mean that every true Christian is covered with an invisible shield of protection whereby the devil can never, under any circumstance touch them. We know this because even the Apostle Peter wasn't safeguarded from the devil touching him! Peter's protection needed his faith and Jesus' prayer.

> **"Simon, Simon! Indeed, Satan has asked for you, that he may sift you as wheat. But I have prayed for you, that your faith should not fail"** (Luke 22:31, 32).

Jesus said that He was free of all demonic control:

> **"I will no longer talk much with you, for the ruler of this world is coming, and he has nothing in Me"** (John 14:30).

Can you say, beyond a shadow of a doubt, that Satan, the "ruler of this world," has nothing in you? To the contrary, Ephesians 4:27 warns us all not to:

> **"give place to the devil."**

The word "place" above in Greek is "topos" which means an area with specific measurements. It is the word from which we get our English word "topography." In some translations it is "foothold." In other words, this "place" is where there is still a measure of uncontrolled territory. A place where a Christian is:

- Possessed by Christ with one area still possessed by the enemy

- A slave of Christ but still chained to one demon

- Fully saved but not fully sanctified

- Free except for that one little zone of bondage

- Set apart by God with an area set apart by the devil

There are Christians who still struggle with pornography, anger, profanity, gossip, hate, unforgiveness, etc. That "topos" may or may not contain a demon. If it is just the flesh, it must be crucified. If it is a demon, it must be cast out. It often is some of each. Hence, the Christian life is both an ongoing learning and growth process, and an ongoing battle.

You can't cast out sin, but you can cast out a demon! Below is proof, a testimony from a nurse in Nebraska:

> "I was a compulsive eater for over forty years. It was nothing for me to eat an entire package of cookies or a pan of brownies at one sitting. I tried every diet I heard of, diet pills, diet clubs, and even hypnosis. As a nurse, I knew the damage I was doing to my body...
>
> **As a Christian** (*Take careful note of that confession!*)
>
> ...I knew I was sinning, but nothing helped. I was depressed, hopeless, and deeply in bondage. When

you prayed for me, I felt a physical and spiritual release. It felt as if a huge, black, toxic core was being pulled from my soul, out through the top of my head. Then I felt the Holy Spirit rush in like a strong wind. The hole left, and the core was filled with the Holy Spirit. It was so powerful, it nearly knocked me over. Since then, I have been completely free of the compulsion and filled with the joy of the Lord. I am exercising regularly, and I feel wonderful. Most importantly, I no longer crave Little Debbie snacks!"

Her mouth was her "topos," but the Lord closed that door from Little Debbie Demons!

1 John 5:10 (NIV) reveals that a "topos" can be drawn by a human "surveyor":

> **"If anyone comes to you and does not bring this teaching, do not take them into your house or welcome them. Anyone who welcomes them shares in their wicked work."**

Christians can unwittingly open their lives to an evil spirit, just as a Christian can open a front door and let a Jehovah's Witness come in to affect their home.

My wife and I recently had to minister deliverance to a Christian woman and her daughter. The mother unwisely allowed her daughter to study with Jehovah's Witnesses. They would come to their house and sit and talk with the girl. One day, she discovered salt inside the *Watchtower* and *Awake* magazines in her bedroom. Other manifestations soon appeared in their home, which required several deliverance sessions. Demons were at work through false teachers invited into a home. I tell the whole story later in the chapter "A Haunted House."

Another verse often used to imply that a Christian can't have a demon is James 3:11 (NKJV):

> **"Does a spring send forth fresh water and bitter from the same opening?"**

James answers his question in v. 10:

> **"Out of the same mouth proceed blessing and cursing. My brethren, these things ought not to be"**

Blessing and cursing coming from the same Christian? They certainly "ought not to be" but they often are, so James adds in v. 9,

> **"With it** (the tongue) **we bless our God and Father, and with it we curse men."**

There is a big difference between something that "ought not to be" and that which is "impossible." If Christians are experiencing blessing and cursing simultaneously, this "ought not to be" and is a call for the deliverance ministry.

Another favorite argument is from 1 Corinthians 6:19:

> **"Do you not know that your body is the temple of the Holy Spirit."**

It is assumed that since the Holy Spirit uses our body as His temple, there couldn't possibly be a demon in that same temple. Jesus was in a synagogue, and a man with a demon was in it also (Luke 4:33). Jesus cast out the demon. Think about it:

Jesus and a demon were in the same "temple."

Satan appeared in the very presence of God in heaven in Job 1, 2. Jesus and Satan were there at the same time. Thank God the day will come when the devil is at last forever "cast out" of heaven (Rev. 12:10). Meanwhile, a lot of Christians on earth need us to help "cast out" demons.

The seemingly paradoxical truth of Christ and a demon in the same body is easier to understand if we think about that fact that man, created in the image of God, is a tripartite being. He has a body, soul, and a spirit. Diseases can invade the body, psychological problems, and demonic spirits can invade the soul, but (THANK GOD!) Jesus reigns supreme through the Holy Spirit in our hearts, the very core of our being.

Consider Paul's word in 1 Thessalonians 5:23:

> **"and may your whole spirit, soul, and body**
> **be preserved blameless at the coming of our**
> **Lord Jesus Christ."**

There is the work of being "preserved" (protected, kept) and "blameless" (without anything that is not of God). Deliverance is one of the tools God uses to do that work.

> **"For the word of God is living and powerful,**
> **and sharper than any two-edged sword,**
> **piercing even to the division of soul and**
> **spirit, and of joints and marrow, and is a**
> **discerner of the thoughts and intents of the**
> **heart. And there is no creature hidden from**
> **His sight"** (Hebrews 4:12, 13).

Demons try to stay hidden in a believer's life, but they can't stay hidden from the Lord. Thus, God gave us His Word and "His sight" (revelation knowledge) to help ferret out these "hidden creatures".

There is often a very fine line "division" of the "soul and the spirit." Deliverance ministers help people by authoritatively applying biblical truth, which can be the "discerner" if there's a hidden demon. The old adage is:

"The man with an opinion is at the mercy of a man with an experience."

I have had hundreds of experiences casting demons out of Christians over a span of four decades. It isn't my opinion; it is my experience: I know that a Christian can have a demon as sure as I know that my name is Dea Warford.

I fought it for years. It didn't seem to make sense. I reasoned,

"How could a Christian be demon-possessed?"

Well, of course, a Christian cannot be demon-possessed, that is, if by demon-possession you mean a demon possesses, controls, and dominates a Christian's entire life. Yet, I have discovered after doing this for over four decades,

A Christian can possess a demon!

Let me give you an illustration. I possess a Citi-bank credit card that probably has a $25,000 limit. I could go down to the bank and get out tens of thousands of dollars cold cash and go on a spending spree. But, as I said, I possess the card. It DOES NOT possess me.

I have a personal friend named B. She was a shopaholic; psychiatrists would say she is an oniomaniac. Oniomania is a medical term for people who have a compulsive need to shop and cannot control that drive.

B. got her family in so much credit card debt that her husband finally had to take her card away from her. She had a credit card that POSSESSED her to the point that her husband had to CAST OUT that card from her purse. A good verse for this principle would be 1 Thessalonians 4:4:

> **"each of you should know how to POSSESS his own vessel in sanctification and honor."**

You might not know that when the Bible says "demon possessed" or "possessed with demons" the Greek Word translated as such is really just one word: "Daimonizomai." The first two definitions of this word in the *Strong's Concordance* are: "to be exercised by a demon" (Oh, is a deliverance session exercise indeed!); and to "have a (be vexed with or possessed with a demon)."

Some translations have expressed the thought of being other than actually "possessed" of a demon. The GNT expresses it as: "people with demons." Other translations simply call those possessed by a demon: "demoniacs." Transliterating the Greek word into English might look like this:

Daimonizomai = Demonized.

As you read the many testimonies in this book you will realize that having a demon doesn't mean the evil spirit completely "possesses" and dominates one's life! Many "demonized" Christians hold down jobs, practice good parenting skills, and are even in the full-time ministry!

If it is still hard for you to believe that a Christian can have a demon, ponder these questions:

1. Can a Christian shoplift and leave a store possessing something in their pocket that has no right to be there? Yes!

2. Can a Christian sleep with a prostitute and afterward possess a venereal disease? Of course!

3. Can a Christian go into a bar and drink and then be possessed with alcohol? No doubt!

4. Can a Christian possess a gun and use it to commit suicide? Tragically some have.

5. Can a Christian buy illegal drugs from a pusher, later be pulled over by a policeman and found guilty of "drug possession?" Absolutely!

Suppose a Christian wanted a demon in his life. Do you think he couldn't have one, no matter how badly he wanted one, just because he's a Christian? I once heard a preacher say,

> **"Can a Christian have a demon? A Christian can have anything he wants!"**

Let me speak more about this from my experience, not my opinion:

- I once ministered deliverance to a woman who said she "liked having a demon around her at her home because she wasn't as lonely and liked the attention!"

- A lady came forward for prayer in one of my services who said, "Pray for me. I needed guidance, so I went to a psychic."

- In New Orleans, a woman came to my evangelistic service in the French Quarter. She came forward for prayer and claimed she was a Christian, yet she read palms to make a living. I told her that she was NOT a Christian and must repent, renounce the occult and start serving the Lord the Bible way. She said that she couldn't that night, but after she paid off her debts, she would. I told her. "Then you will never be out of debt" (the devil is a cruel and relentless taskmaster!)!

Christians make their choices in life, and they pay the consequences. And after many, many deliverance sessions, I assure you that carrying around a demon is often one of these consequences.

You might ask,

"How can Jesus and a demon dwell in the same body?"

Let me answer that question with two questions:

1. How can Jesus and a sin dwell in the same body?

2. How can Jesus and cancer dwell in the same body?

Didn't Jesus die to deliver us from sins, and didn't He shed his blood to deliver us from cancer? Yes, indeed! Neither sin nor disease has a right to stay in our body, nor does a demon (yet many Christians are wrestling with both!). Demons are like home squatters which have no legal right to stay in someone else's home.

To get a squatter out of a home requires going to court and getting a legal document declaring that the squatter will be removed by a Marshal at such and such a date. Similarly, go to the courts of heaven, discover your legal document (Promises in His Word), and then YOU be the Marshal and remove that demon from a house (body).

Demons are spirits, so they can pass through walls. A haunted house is a house where demons have passed through walls and stayed there. Well, if they can pass through a plaster wall, don't you think they can pass through skin? And if they can pass through skin into a body, don't you think they can stop for a moment, or a day or for even years, that is, when a 'topos" is available to them?

It might help to compare ourselves with the Old Testament Temple, since 1 Corinthians 9:19 says:

"Your body is the Temple of the Holy Spirit."

The Temple was comprised of an outer court, an inner court, and the Holy Place. The outer court can be likened to our body, the inner court to our souls, and the Holy Place to our heart, inner man, or spirit.

The High Priest was the only one who could enter the Holy Place. Heb. 3:1 informs us that Jesus is our High Priest. He entered our heart to reign as our Lord and Savior. But other priests, even unsaved ones, could enter the other areas of the Temple. Demons can do likewise, entering our bodies or our souls.

"I pray that Christ will make his home in your hearts through faith" (Ephesians 3:17 GNT).

If Christ has made His home in our hearts, we must keep the faith that He will continue to reign supreme there. If other areas of our life (evil beings rooted in our body or soul) are seeking to supplant His Lordship, that's a call for some spiritual housecleaning.

I spoke in a church in Covina, California. I discovered that the pastor must not have believed a Christian could have a demon. I should have known, since he was part of a denomination that officially taught that Christians can't have a demon. Following my sermon, a woman, probably in her fifties, came up for prayer.

As I started waging spiritual warfare on her behalf, with the pastor closely watching my actions, the woman cried, "I won't come out!" The pastor stepped over to where I was and told me, "She's faking it." He had assumed, since she was a Christian, that she couldn't possibly have a demon, therefore she must have been faking it.

Can you imagine a Christian woman in her fifties saying during prayer, "I won't come out!" I can't either. It was a demon speaking through her voice. That pastor may have prayed for her often, preached to her, and counseled her. But that didn't get the demon out. It took the deliverance ministry. (Incidentally, that same pastor left his wife and the ministry, and last I heard he was playing the guitar in a bar. I can't help but wonder if the deliverance ministry could have helped him).

The last thing the devil wants Christians to know is that he might be behind their problems! In conclusion, are you dealing with the flesh or the devil, a sin or a demon? My take on the subject is:

WHEN IN DOUBT, CAST IT OUT!

12

I Don't Think; I Know!

"For we cannot but speak the things which we have seen and heard" (Acts 4:20).

Following is a testimony from a beautiful Christian woman, one that I have come to know along with her husband:

"The idea of demons has never startled me because I grew up hearing about them all the time. My mother always told me that her mother had demons. My great-grandmother was a fortune teller. She reportedly carried the Bible in one pocket and tarot cards in the other. That bondage has continued, apparently, even to me. While listening to you Sunday morning, I knew there was something I needed delivered from but had no idea, really. I forgave my mother and was delivered from a demon that had been bestowed upon me since birth. Jesus is the Lord of my life and I am a child of the Most High God, which left me befuddled after my encounter with you and my deliverance from a demon. How could I have a demon and be filled with the Holy Spirit at the same time? I came home after church and opened my Bible looking for a word. I opened to Jeremiah 30:8-11, "In that day . . . I will break the yoke off their necks and tear off their bonds: no longer will foreigners enslave them. . .so do not fear, O Jacob (I saw my name) do not be dismayed. . .declares the Lord. . .Jacob (Me) will again have peace and security, and no one will make him (me) afraid. I am with you and will save you,' declares the Lord.'" Jesus has delivered me and my descendants."

If you had sat beside me at altars and in prayer rooms in church after church around the nation spanning decades and had witnessed what I have, you could not deny what you had "seen and heard" (Acts 4:20). If you saw Christian after Christian (like the above Christian), faithful church members who love Jesus, coughing, gagging, screaming and fighting as I took authority over their demons and then afterward heard their testimonies of the dramatic change in their lives, you would believe just like I do! You would believe that a Christian can have a demon and need deliverance.

If you do believe, "A Christian cannot have a demon," then I need to ask you a question. "Have you ever cast a demon out of a sinner?" To my knowledge:

I have never cast a demon out of a sinner.

Think about it! What good would it do for me to go into a bar and cast a demon out of some drunk? After I left, he'd likely just say, "Hey, fellas, I just got religion! The next round is on me!"

Some Christians just haven't thought this through! If a Christian can't have a demon, then we don't need the deliverance ministry. Why? Because if a Christian can't have a demon, all we need to do is lead a sinner to Christ, and then immediately, the demon would have to leave.

I have led many hundreds to the Lord through the years, and not once did I have to cast a demon out before they could get saved. Have you? Has your pastor? Has any evangelist that you know?

It's not that we can't cast a demon out of an unsaved person. It's just that deliverance from demons is not intended for sinners. They don't want to serve Christ and be delivered from their bondage. Deliverance is for drunks who leave the bar and come to church longing to be delivered and are happy to repent and invite Jesus to come into their life. After this proof of sincerity, the church can cast out that spirit of bondage!

When a foreigner came to Christ asking Him to cast the demon out of her daughter, Jesus told her:

> **"it is not right to take the children's bread and toss it to the dogs"** (Mark 7:27 NIV).

Deliverance is "the children's bread." Christ extended grace to a desperate sinner that day, but He also made it clear that such things were still primarily for the children of God.

A man was filled with demons who were tormenting him. Concerned citizens had bound him in chains where he lived in a graveyard. Night and day, he would cry and cut himself with stones. But then Jesus came:

> **"When he saw Jesus a long way off, he ran and bowed in worship before him"** (Mark 5:6 MSG).

This man wanted to be free, and he believed Jesus could help him. The first thing he did when he saw Jesus was to run toward him and worship him! Now that speaks volumes! He was bound, but he wasn't a Christ-rejector! He was a Christ-acceptor, and such are candidates to be made free!

A fortune-telling woman believed in Jesus. The Bible says that she followed Paul. She testified in Acts 16:17:

> **"These are the servants of God who show us the way of salvation."**

She did this "MANY days." She wasn't rejecting Christ. She was seeking Him and attending to Paul's teachings. She was still bound. Eventually, Paul discerned the demon hiding inside her life and cast it out (read about it in Acts 16:16-18).

Paul wrote a letter to a church; thus, it was written with Christians in mind. He told them in 1 Corinthians 10:20:

> **"the things which the Gentiles sacrifice they sacrifice to demons and not to God, and I do not want you to have fellowship with demons."**

I have had to minister to many Christians who had "fellowship with demons." Below is a testimony I received from a Timothy S:

> "I was a professional stage hypnotist who was stricken with a dilemma about what I was doing for a living. Was it right or wrong in God's eyes? My answer came quite unexpectedly after a brother in Christ invited me to a breakfast at the church I not so frequently attend. Dea Warford's sermon was on deliverance from sin. Two days earlier, I was having a conflict with going back to church because of what I felt the church body thought of my hypnosis career. After the meeting, I was talking to Dea regarding

hypnosis. He shed a new light on this, which I know now to be an evil practice. I now know the dangers that follow it. I sat in a chair rebuking and repenting for all the sins I had committed, knowingly and unknowingly, through this practice. I began seeing things in a new light. When Dea cast this demon with the "talent" of hypnosis out of me, I felt the presence leave me! Glory to God. Afterward I felt a peace in my heart that I had never felt before. I KNOW that the practice of hypnosis is an evil art, and this has given me the strength and the conviction that God has better things in mind for me. Praise Jesus!"

Christians can receive a demon:

> **"For if he who comes preaches another Jesus whom we have not preached, or if you receive a different spirit which you have not received, or a different gospel which you have not accepted — you may well put up with it"** (2 Cor. 11:3)!

Paul wrote this verse to Christians. He makes it very clear that it is possible to "receive a different spirit." You can "receive" the Spirit of Christ into your home (Revelation 3:20) and subsequently keep the door shut to all others. Or you can open the door to "different" kinds of other spirits and foolishly "receive" them into your home, your mind, or your body.

A certain Christian man in the same Corinthian church had been sleeping with his mother-in-law. Paul warned the church to:

> **"deliver such a one to Satan for the destruction of the flesh, that his spirit may be saved in the day of the Lord Jesus"** (1 Cor. 5:5).

Your spirit can be saved, yet at the same time, your body may be destroyed by Satan and his evil emissaries.

Christians are puzzled about the geography of demons. Are they in a person, on a person, or just around a person? Does it really matter? I don't want a thief at my window, in my living room, in bed with me, or on top of me with a knife at my throat! I don't want him anywhere near me, and I will do my best to cast that thief out of my life! And the same goes for demons.

Cast demons out of houses, off shoulders, out of minds, out of stomachs, off backs, whenever and wherever they might happen to be. Demons are invisible unless God allows them to manifest or enables one to see into the spirit world through the gift of discerning of spirits. I have never seen a demon. Some have, but they describe them in many different ways.

Could it be possible that demons are in a different dimension than we are. Is this science fiction fantasy? Think for a moment about heaven and the throne of God. Is it above the sky for people in America, thus down beneath for those in China? Or is it above for people in China and down for Americans? Is it trillions of miles away or right here among us, just in a different dimension?

Consider also, can a demon's anatomy be comprehended by our natural mind? For instance, can you envision how "legion" (several thousand demons) could live in one person (See Luke 8:30)? Do they shrink to the size of an ant so they can all fit in? Do they stack inside of one another as some Russian stacking doll? It's a mystery.

We are not even sure what demons are because the Bible doesn't clarify that for us. Some believe they are fallen angels. Others believe that they are the disembodied spirits of a pre-adamic race. Perhaps they were the cavemen killed along with the dinosaurs, and God let their spirits wander on earth, deciding to use them later to train us? This is interesting to consider but not important.

If you are interested in my opinion of the matter: I think the weight of evidence is that these demons are fallen angels. We know that one-third of the heavenly angels rebelled with Satan and followed him to the planet earth:

> **"His tail drew a third of the stars of heaven
> and threw them to the earth"** (Revelation 12:4).

In addition, Jesus said in Mark 3:23:

> **"How can Satan cast out Satan?"**

That the Lord would refer to casting out a demon as actually casting out Satan shows how closely aligned demons are with Satan. This suggests that these evil spirits possessing humans are at least a percentage of the fallen angels. Satan could have assigned such angels to this very purpose. Other angels would then be referred to in Ephesians 6:12 NIV:

> **"For our struggle is not against flesh and
> blood, but against the rulers, against the
> authorities, against the powers of this dark
> world and against the spiritual forces of evil
> in the heavenly realms."**

I don't know if it is still the case today, but at one time in Germany, high schoolers would all take a test. Those who scored highest would go on to college and those who scored lower would instead be sent to trade schools. Similarly, Satan might have assigned the weaker, less apt angels to the dirty deed of possession (Just a thought).

Come to your own conclusions. Yet, where a thief was born, how smart or strong he is, or what he looks like would not at all be important to me! I don't like thieves, wherever they are from, or whatever they are like. And I don't like demons, wherever they are from and whatever they actually are.

Face to Face

Evil Spirits can contort a person's face, showing ferocity or hatred as if they were about to kill you. When I first started casting out demons, I went through a period of fear. It wasn't that I doubted my authority over any demon, but it was just the thought that as I was walking across the living room to use the bathroom in the middle of the night, one might pop out from behind the sofa and, for a moment, terrorize me!

I knew after I responded, "In, in, in, the Na, Na, Name of J, J, Jesus, GO!" they would have to do so, yet I still dreaded such a moment happening. It didn't take many deliverance sessions for that fear to dissipate. Demons would speak through someone's mouth saying such things as: "We don't like you," "Please don't cast us out" or moan, "NO!" I soon realized:

> **"Hallelujah! I don't have to be afraid of
> demons! They are afraid of me!"**

Some Christians stumble by visualizing demons as Hollywood movies have depicted them: huge monstrous beings, tossing priests out windows, or climbing across ceilings. If demons are fallen angels, I can tell you by experience that those angels fell very hard (just as mankind did!).

It is estimated that humans use 10% of our brain (A result of the fall?). "Fallen" demons also don't seem to possess a lot of intelligence. One time I was casting demons out of a woman and the demons spoke through her voice and said, "We're going!" Then, a moment later, they spoke again through her and said, "We're gone!" If they were gone, then how could they still speak through her voice? How dumb did they think I was?

Demons show great fear and weakness when challenged by a Spirit-filled, Jesus exalting believer. They will lie and "fake it" for a while to see if they can scare you away. Let me assure you after dealing with hundreds, if not thousands of them:

Demons are much more like a cockroach than they are a monster.

Cockroaches hide in the darkness of a room. When the light is turned on and they are exposed, we stomp on them! When demons are revealed, do the same!

Following is a testimony from Brian S. in New Jersey:

"I attend the Abundant Life Church. I have had deep-seated anger. My wife says it manifests itself like the incredible hulk (he clinched his fists and his muscles flexed as his face glared furiously). I am a Bible-believing, pew jumping, praise warrior, and intercessor with my church. I didn't even believe that anything like that could come upon me. Dea was praying that any spirit would manifest itself. It took about five minutes, then suddenly, I started growling and went from the pew to my knees. Dea said I had to repent of the anger. I did and released it. My body started contorting, flailing, and kicking. When Dea left to pray for someone else, the pastor and some intercessors came over and began praying for me. It left and went out screaming. It was nasty. I felt clean and so at peace. My countenance even changed."

Did you catch that? This testimony was from:

"a Bible believing, pew jumping, praise warrior and intercessor with my church."

If Brian were not a real Christian, how can we know if you, I, or anyone else is truly a Christian?

Here is another testimony from Betty B. of South Dakota.

"I was demon-possessed over twenty-five years ago before I was a Christian. I saw a movie about demon possession. I told the pastor at the church where I first got saved, 'I think that might be me.' He said, 'No, you're too sweet.' It changed in a matter of minutes. My sweetness was gone. The pastor cast out that one demon. We thought that was all there was. I have loved God for over twenty-five years, loved Him, and served Him. I have been a women's leader, and I prophesied. So, I thought it was all behind me. Then, on Thursday night, as Dea was praying for others, I felt nausea whenever he commanded any hidden demons to manifest themselves. As they began praying for me, the demons began to throw me. They began to be more violent. There were several times I thought I was going to die! I thought, 'They have got to stop because I am not going to make it.' There seemed to be more and more. Some of them seemed to speak to me that they didn't want to leave. There was one in particular. He was 'Resentment.' He said, 'I am not leaving. I have been here a long time. I am not going!' And, I think he was probably the last one to go. But he is gone! Finally, I felt clean and transparent. I think you could shine a flashlight through me. I felt so free."

I remind you of Betty's confession of faith:

"I have loved God for over twenty-five years, loved Him, and served Him. I have been a women's leader, and I prophesied."

The Warford's Demon

Are you still not convinced that a Christian can have a demon? Perhaps my personal story about an experience with my wife, Kathy, will convince you:

We were pastoring a church in Hawaiian Gardens, California. We lived in the parsonage next door to the church with our two young children. There was a couple across the street who got drunk one night. They got into a big fight, (and one of them must have said, "Well, let's go tell Pastor, burp, Dea about it!"). They were soon yelling at each other in our front yard. I stood on the front porch, trying to console them.

Kathy was beside herself! It was 9 PM. Our kids were in bed. Those drunks were disturbing our peace. She thought I should have been "a man" about it and made them both go home and offer to counsel with them tomorrow after they had slept it off.

Instead, like a good pastor, I patiently tried to reason with them. Kathy couldn't take it anymore. Just inside the front door, she began to flail at me with her fists! I grabbed her arms (to protect both her and me) and wrestled her to the ground. Immediately her back began to hurt. She calmed down a little as the couple finally left. Her back still hurt. It bothered her through the night. When she awakened in the morning, her back still hurt. Then the Lord spoke to her and said:

"It's a demon!"

She told me what the Lord had told her, and so I said, "OK, let's cast it out." We took authority over a demon and commanded it to leave in Jesus' Name! It did, right away, and her back pain immediately stopped.

I was a pastor who let a demon into his house, and a Spirit-filled pastor's wife then had a demon enter her body. Note: it only came out after we commanded it to leave! Demons don't slip out because you are so sweet!

A courtroom full of theologians could not convince Martin Luther to recant his justification by faith theology. Likewise, a courtroom full of preachers couldn't get me to recant my theology of deliverance.

But thank God, you and I can cast em' out! So, if a Christian can have a demon, how in the world did it ever enter in the first place? We'll answer that question in the next chapter (That is, if you haven't tossed this book into the trash yet...like the devil would love you to do! Oh, and you simply MUST at least read Chapters 15 and 19 before you throw it away!).

In finishing up this chapter, let me be as blunt as I can.

"I don't think a Christian can have a demon . . .

I KNOW a Christian can have a demon!"

13

Sin And Evil Spirits

"To this end the Son of God has been manifested, that he might undo the works of the devil" (1 John 3:8 DBY).

The germ theory of disease was but one answer posited as the reason for deadly diseases that killed so many. It took three scientific discoveries to prove the idea was accurate and to provide an effective solution. Though other contemporaries were involved, there are three men most attributed with these discoveries:

1. Antonie Van Leeuwenhoek is most credited with the invention of the microscope (though others were also involved). His discovery of microscopic organisms in about 1666 was a giant step forward in medicine.

2. Louis Pasteur in the 1850s' observed with a microscope and postulated the germ theory of disease, which proved to be the exact cause of the origin and spreading of many deadly diseases throughout history.

3. Alexander Fleming in 1928, discovered the first true antibiotic, penicillin.

The Word of God is your microscope to "see" into the realm of what is invisible to the naked eye, germs (demons). And your antibiotic is the Blood and Name of Jesus.

Do you suspect that you or someone you know might need deliverance from an evil spirit? Let's look together into the "microscope" of God's Word to see what is behind spiritual infection.

Paul lists the nine fruits of the spirit in Galatians 5:22, 23. When the Holy Spirit is operating in our life, and our spirit is being nurtured and is growing, these fruits will increasingly be produced in us. In the same way, if the enemy is operating in our life, we will be experiencing a certain kind of "fruit." Jesus said:

> **"You will know them by their fruits"**
> (Matthew 7:16).

We are personally responsible to know which spirit we are in tune with.

> **"Beloved, do not believe every spirit, but**
> **TEST the spirits, whether they are of God"**
> (1 John 4:1).

We can test spirits by the Word of God, and also by the fruit they bear. Consider the clear contrast between the fruit of the spirit in Galatians 5:22,23 (KJV) and the opposite fruit of an unholy spirit.

The Fruit of the Spirit	The Fruit of an unholy spirit
Love	Hate, bitterness
Joy	Depression, Suicidal thoughts
Peace	Torment, Condemnation, anxiety
Longsuffering	Unforgiveness, resentment
Gentleness	Anger, violence, abuse
Goodness	Uncleanness, lust, lying, gossip
Faith	Fear, rejection, self-pity
Meekness	Pride, criticism, judgmentalism
Self-control	Bad habits, obsessions, compulsions

None are perfected yet in the fruit of the spirit and we all have times when we are guilty of producing the fruit of the unholy spirit. However, if you discover these evil fruits perfectly describe someone, if they are growing and clinging to them, or are monopolizing areas of their life, we have the microscope of James 3:15-18 shedding much light on the subject:

> **"But if you have bitter envy and self-seeking in your hearts, do not boast and lie against the truth. This wisdom does not descend from above, but is earthly, sensual, demonic. For where envy and self-seeking exist, confusion and every evil thing are there. But the wisdom that is from above is first pure, then peaceable, gentle, willing to yield, full of mercy and good fruits, without partiality and without hypocrisy. Now the fruit of righteousness is sown in peace by those who make peace."**

The fruit of the spirit results from "the wisdom that is from above...full of...good fruits." When the opposite fruit is growing, Verse 15 says it is "demonic." The fruit of the spirit is the natural outgrowth of receiving the Holy Spirit into our lives and living by His divine enablement. If an evil spirit is producing his fruit instead, we must get rid of him.

Paul wrote to the Christians at Rome and said:

> **"For you did not receive the spirit of bondage again to fear, but you received the Spirit of adoption"** (Romans 8:15).

Paul used the same terminology ("receive") for acquiring a demon ("the spirit of bondage") as He did receiving the Spirit of God. This gives us many clues as to how someone can "receive" an evil spirit. The comparison is fascinating.

How to receive the Holy Spirit or an evil spirit

Holy Spirit: You listen to and heed the instructions of a teacher or preacher.

evil spirit: You listen to and heed the instructions of evil men or are bruised by their evil words.

Holy Spirit: You fulfill the scriptural requirements, "the Holy Spirit whom God has given to those who obey Him" (Acts 5:32).

evil spirit: You fulfill the scriptural requirements (sin, disobeying God's Word).

Holy Spirit: You ask to receive the Holy Spirit, "How much more will your heavenly Father give the Holy Spirit to those who ask Him" (Luke 11:13).

evil spirit: You "ask" for an unholy spirit by submitting yourself to a psychic, dabbling in the occult, etc. (and I have actually had some admit that they had asked the devil to come into their life!).

Holy Spirit: Spirit-filled friends lay hands on and encourage you, and speak words from God's Word over you.

evil spirit: Unholy people lay hands on you, hurt you, influence you, and speak words from hell over you (see Matthew 4, Luke 4, Mark 8:33).

Holy Spirit: You believe the promises of God's Word.

evil spirit: You believe the lies of people or the enemy.

Holy Spirit: You receive the Holy Spirit (Acts 19:6).

evil spirit: You receive an evil spirit (2 Cor. 11:4).

A demon doesn't just walk into a person's life at the drop of a hat. Ecclesiastes 10:8 (NIV) gives us an interesting metaphor that is apropos:

> **"Whoever digs a pit may fall into it; whoever breaks through a wall may be bitten by a snake."**

Demons need an invitation. Digging pits or walls broken through refer to a place and time "falls" or "bites" begin. That fall could be a violation of a law of God! That "bite" could start with a mental suggestion. If that thought is "received" and allowed to take root, it can become a "place" a "topos" that Satan can then occupy. This is what happened to Judas:

"And supper being ended, the devil having already put it into the heart of Judas Iscariot, Simon's son, to betray Him... Now after the piece of bread, Satan entered him" (John 13:2, 27).

Satan suggested betrayal to Judas, who accepted that thought into his heart. He never repented of it or asked for deliverance. Finally, Satan himself (Not just a demon!) entered him! (I believe Satan himself will possess the coming Antichrist!). Satan's suggestion is what got this whole snowball rolling:

"But I fear, lest somehow, as the serpent deceived Eve by his craftiness, so your minds may be corrupted from the simplicity (singleness of heart) **that is in Christ"** (2 Cor. 11:3).

The mind is the battlefield. Satan told Eve that she wouldn't die. It was a lie. He deceived her into disobeying God. The fall resulted. But through spiritual warfare we can get back on track spiritually:

"For the weapons of our warfare are not carnal but mighty in God for pulling down strongholds, casting down arguments and... bringing every thought into captivity to the obedience of Christ" (2 Cor. 10:4, 5).

Thoughts are what spiritual warfare is all about. Satan's lies, when believed, allow the enemy to build a **"stronghold"** (a place he occupies) in a life. **"Casting down arguments"** can picture a Christian in bondage determined to no longer believe the Devil's lies. Then, God calls us to bring that thought, that lie, **"...to the obedience of Christ."**

Obedience is what repentance is all about. Repentance means a change of mind and a change of direction. When someone who is in bondage to sin or Satan makes up their mind that they don't want that sin or that demon in their life anymore, they will obey Christ. They will start taking the necessary steps to change their direction; they are on their way to deliverance.

Deliverance ministers must be:

> **"gentle as you correct your opponents, for it may be that God will give them the opportunity to repent and come to know the truth. And then they will come to their senses and escape from the trap of the Devil, who had caught them and made them obey his will"** (2 Tim. 2:25, 26 GNT).

The above primarily addresses our ministry to the unsaved, but the principles also apply in dealing with Christians bound in "the trap of the Devil." Note the words:

"gentle" (Love the sinner, hate the sin).

"correct" (Use the truth of the Word to show why they are caught in that trap).

"the opportunity to repent" (They will have to repent of things they have done or attitudes that kept them in bondage).

"escape" (Another word for being delivered).

"obey his will" (It is a call to The Lord's Prayer in Matthew 6:9-13, where we pray. . .

"Your will be done" (Which is a surrender to the Lord's will, and His will only), followed by the prayer to,

"Deliver us from evil"

They are called "evil spirits." Christians deal with them, in one way or another, every day. It is the word **"stronghold"** from 2 Corinthians 10:4 that is a summons for deliverance ministers. There are several primary strongholds we need to examine in this chapter and the following chapter. These are "the works of the devil" that Christ came to "undo" as expressed in 1 John 3:8 (DBY).

Stronghold #1: Sin

"they allure through the lusts of the flesh, through licentiousness, While they promise them liberty, they themselves are slaves of corruption: for by WHOM a person is overcome, by him also he is brought into bondage" (2 Peter 2:18, 19).

What starts as an "allurement" to sins of "the flesh" can ultimately become a bondage to a living being. "Whom," in this context, speaks of false human prophets, but bondage to actual demons often follows sin.

There are degrees of evil. Some sins are worse than others. Even sinful humankind acknowledges this truth, as it punishes some evil acts more than others with varying degrees of jail time or even capital punishment. Jesus said that the Jews who delivered him to Pilate had committed a "greater sin" than Pilate.

There are also varying degrees of punishment in hell (See Luke 12:47, 48; Romans 2:5; Revelation 20:12).

What starts as just a manifestation of a sin of the flesh can become a stronghold for increasingly greater demonic control. Paul calls bitterness a root that,

"springing up cause trouble, and by this many become defiled" (Hebrews 12:15).

Any sin can "spring up" and become a root of evil. There are some more severe sins, however, that are proven to be a probable cause of indwelling demonic bondage.

I was ministering deliverance to a woman in New Mexico. She kept manifesting a demonic presence by her body language, but I couldn't seem to get her free. I usually don't ask people about sins in their life until I have to (most Christians live under such condemnation for their failures that they don't need an evangelist to rub it in more!). Their sin is usually under the blood anyway, as they love Jesus, hate the sin, and confess it time and time again.

After exhausting other causes for her bondage, I finally asked her, "Do you have any sin in your life that you haven't yet fully repented of?" She did.

Her husband was in the military and stationed in the Middle East. She admitted that, while he was away, she would sleep with any man who would come to her house bringing her candy or flowers. I explained that she had to ask the Lord to forgive her and make a commitment never to do it again (which is what true repentance is!). After she willingly did this, the demon came out shortly with very little manifestation (a proven sign of a fully-accomplished surrender to the Lord).

Bondage to sin through alcoholism, drug addiction, sexual sin, or other obsessive-compulsive behaviors can be demonically induced or at least greatly exacerbated by demons. Here's a testimony from Tawnee in Alaska:

"I had tried to serve God most of my life. I always failed. I had a nervous breakdown. I started to drink every day. I lost everything I had worked for in 16 years of marriage. Within two months, I was homeless. I started drinking at the age of twelve (I am thirty-seven now). I would smoke hundreds of dollar's worth of crack almost every night with friends. For two years, I wanted to die all the time. In my brief periods of not drinking, I would read Psalm 91:14, where God said that because I had set my love on Him, He would deliver me. That was my only hope. I hadn't been in church for two years. I don't drive, and the few times I had wanted to go to church, I couldn't find a ride. That night something very special happened when you and Kathy prayed for me. Almost two weeks later, as I walked by my drug dealer's house, I realized I had been delivered. I hadn't thought of drinking or using drugs. They were so far gone from my mind; I didn't realize I'd been totally set free for two weeks! My mind is cleansed in other ways too. I no longer want to die. The self-hatred is gone! I was also obsessed with men and sex, my idea of love, just so that someone would love me. It was a very big problem in my life. It's gone! No obsession! It's clean. I'm free, free to serve God, body, soul, and spirit. My mind is clean. Before, I couldn't control my thoughts. Now I can! If my mind gets off track, I can tell my mind to think holy thoughts. God set me free!

I should add to this story that as Kathy and I began to pray over her, she soon cried aloud, "It's hopeless! It's hopeless! It's hopeless!" (I had never sensed such hopelessness in my life!). Then a demon inside her cried out:

"She's mine!"

I shot back,

"She's Jesus'!"

Again,

"She's mine!"

I retorted,

"She's Jesus'!"

This Hollywood movie scene went back and forth for a while (at rapid-fire!). After maybe a half-hour of taking dominion, at last, the demons were gone. She wrote us the above testimony two weeks later.

Demons will take full advantage of sin. It is certainly a stronghold we must fight against. The simple rule of thumb is:

SIN is a NO, NO!

14

Unforgiveness And Witchcraft

**"lest Satan should take advantage of us; for we
are not ignorant of his devices"**
(2 Corinthians 2:11)

Stronghold #2 Unforgiveness

After decades of ministering deliverance to Christians,
probably the most pervasive problem they struggle with is
unforgiveness and related bitterness, hatred, and deep-rooted
anger. Jesus taught us to pray:

"deliver us from the evil one" (Matthew 6:13).

Then added in Verse 14:

> **"For if you forgive men their trespasses, your
> heavenly Father will also forgive you. But if you
> do not forgive men their trespasses, neither will
> your Father forgive your trespasses."**

If we want to be delivered from demons, we have to forgive others...PERIOD! I do not believe when it says the Father won't forgive you that it means if you don't perfectly forgive every person who throughout your lifetime has hurt you, you will go to hell. I have met too many wonderful Christians who loved the Lord with all their heart but just couldn't quite forgive and forget the pain others through the years had brought them.

It is not so much the person's stubborn refusal to forgive as it is a repeated demonic reminder, tormenting them again and again, haunting them with memories from their troubled past.

Luke 18:21-35 throws further light on this. Jesus told a parable about a man who was forgiven of a great debt by his master. Later the same man refused to forgive someone who owed him a much smaller amount. After hearing about this refusal to forgive:

> **"Then his master, after he had called him, said to him, 'You wicked servant! I forgave you all that debt because you begged me. Should you not also have had compassion on your fellow servant, just as I had pity on you? And his master was angry, and delivered him to the TORTURERS until he should pay all that was due him. So My heavenly Father also will do to you if each of you, from his heart, does not forgive his brother his trespasses.' "**

The word "torturers" is "tormentors" in the Authorized Version. This is a difficult verse to interpret, and not necessary for this limited study, but one thing is sure:

> **Unforgiveness can subjugate one to torture and torment, both self-inflicted and demonically-inflicted.**

When I pastored in Hawaiian Gardens, CA, there was a woman once in my office who confided that her husband had sexually molested her daughter. Of course, it destroyed their marriage. Her face, though quite pretty, showed advancing signs of premature aging from long torment (The stress hormone, cortisol, is called "the ugly hormone" as it actually makes a person appear less attractive. It also destroys one's health!).

She had never forgiven her husband who had done such evil to her daughter. In fact, she told me:

"If I had three whole days to torture him, it wouldn't be enough!"

I said, "But you have to forgive him." She retorted, "I can't." I repeated, "You HAVE to forgive him!" She fled from my office crying:

"I can't, I can't!"

Truly a "root of bitterness springing up" had "defiled" her (Hebrews 12:15). What her husband did was horribly wrong and deserving of punishment. However, the mistake she made was trying to punish him in her mind. She made herself his judge, jury, and longed as well to be his executioner. She too committed a great sin. She refused, by a stubborn act of her will, to submit to the words of our Lord to forgive.

She ran away from the Lord instead of towards him. She was being tormented by the memory of her husband's actions and tortured by demonic powers whom she had allowed access into her life. It is such a sad story.

On the other hand, how beautiful it is when we forgive. Below is a testimony from Tampa, Florida. This strong Christian woman had been molested by her father:

> "I have a testimony of deliverance. I thought I had been healed concerning the molestation previous to this night, but I was to find out I was wrong. I had perverted thoughts for many years, unable to see a father and daughter together without thinking of the past or believing they could have a pure relationship. You called out a spirit of shame, a spirit of uncleanness, a spirit of self-hatred and a tormenting spirit. Nearly twenty years had gone by that I had neither seen or talked to my dad who had molested me as I entered into my teenager years. At the end of my teenager years, I ran away from home. Years later I did visit my parents, but I never felt comfortable around my dad. It was always awkward. I always felt shame, unclean, and worse. I put on weight so I wouldn't be attractive (this was before I knew the Lord). After your meeting at our church, I had to go see my dad for the first time in almost twenty years. Because of your ministry and God's faithfulness to His Word, I was able to kiss my dad's forehead, and touch the now very old, wrinkled, dry skin and the bruised and shrunken hands that had molested me so many years ago. I was able to spend time in his presence alone without shame, resentment, disgust or any one of those awful emotions or thoughts that had plagued me for many years. I was able to touch him with love, tenderness, and compassion, and to tell my dad I love him. So complete was the Lord's healing and deliverance!"

A man in the church at Corinth had committed a grievous sin. He was disfellowshipped from the local church at the direction of Apostle Paul (see 1 Corinthians 5:1-5). Apparently, the man had later truly repented, and Paul wrote to the church that they should now "forgive and comfort him" (2 Corinthians 2:7). Paul explained why in his second epistle to that church in 2 Corinthians 2:10 (GNT):

> **"When you forgive people for what they have done, I forgive them too. For when I forgive - if, indeed, I need to forgive anything - I do it in Christ's presence because of you."**

Then Paul explains why it is important to forgive in the next verse:

> **"lest Satan should take advantage of us; for we are not ignorant of his devices."**

Unforgiveness is a powerful "device" of the devil, but forgiveness is infinitely more powerful. It is also an absolute must to obtain complete freedom. We'll see how easy it is to forgive in teaching ahead.

Stronghold #3: The Occult, Witchcraft and False Religions

Any attempt to enter the invisible/supernatural realm except through Jesus and/or the Word of God is to enter the demonic realm. Acts 16:16 speaks of:

> **"a certain slave girl possessed with a spirit of divination."**

Divination is the practice of seeking to divine things unknown or unseeable to the naked eye or to determine future events. The verse continues:

> **"who brought her masters much profit by fortune-telling."**

The modern term "psychic" describes this practice. The Old Testament also speaks of those possessed with the powers of the occult:

> **"Then Saul said to his servants, "Find me a woman who is a medium, that I may go to her and inquire of her." And his servants said to him, "In fact, there is a woman who is a medium at En Dor. So Saul disguised himself and put on other clothes, and he went, and two men with him; and they came to the woman by night. And he said, "Please conduct a seance for me, and bring up for me the one I shall name to you"** (1 Samuel 28:7, 8).

Mediums CANNOT "bring up" the spirits of the dead. It is a deception and if there are any supposed appearances, you can be sure that it is a just a demon. That is why the word medium above is translated in other translations as "familiar spirit."

If a medium tried to conjure up Charlie Manson, for instance, she would only be conjuring up a demon who might be somewhat familiar with Charlie (Maybe even possessing him at one time!). Thus, that demon might imitate Charlie's voice and answer questions which would seem to prove to onlookers that the spirit was actually Charlie Manson.

> **"Satan himself transforms himself into an angel of light"** (2 Corinthians 11:14).

Joseph Smith thought that an angel named "Moroni" was appearing to him to help him write the Book of Mormon. We know that angel was satanic.

The founder of Islam, Muhammed, was visited by a being who said he was the angel "Gabriel." This "angel of light" demon helped Muhammed write the Koran.

The modern-day psychic, Jeane Dixon (b. 1904, d. 1997), claimed she was given a crystal ball by a gypsy when she was a girl. The gypsy prophesied that Jean would become a famous seer. Later Jeane reported that she had a vision of a black and yellow snake that coiled around her body and looked her into the eyes. She felt no fear, only peace.

Jeane was deceived as all psychics are. She claimed to be a Christian, a Catholic, and felt that her "gift" was a gift from God. It's somewhat surprising that she couldn't make the connection between the snake that visited her and the serpent in the garden who deceived Eve.

> **"But I fear that somehow your pure and undivided DEVOTION TO CHRIST will be corrupted, just as Eve was deceived by the cunning ways of the serpent"** (2 Corinthians 11:3 NLT).

"Devotion to Christ" is our call. All forms of the occult, witchcraft, and false religions are tools demons use to recruit devotion to them.

> **"the things which the Gentiles sacrifice they sacrifice to demons and not to God, and I do not want you to have fellowship with demons"** (1 Corinthians 10:20).

Demons use idols as a contact point with people. The same could be said of crystal balls, Ouija boards, tarot cards, or any other physical object that demons use to make a connection with human spirits. Following is a testimony I received from Donna H.,

> "From the time that I was a little kid I loved anything native American and always rooted for the Indians in the cowboy movies. . .

(Quick interjection from Dea: I was watching a TV Western when my young son, Nathan, came in just as cowboys were chasing Indians and firing their pistols. My son reported gleefully, "Dad, when I grow up, I want to be a cowboy and shoot Indians!" Cute, but NOT AT ALL politically correct!)

> . . .As I grew up I really got into the Indian stuff. I gave my life to the Lord at a Foursquare Church in Montana. I removed my medicine bag from around my neck and hung it on the wall. I began my walk with the Lord, but things were happening. My house was filled with noises, especially at night. I kept seeing flitting shadows. I had the house prayed over twice and it would quiet down for a while but not for long. The third time, I became frightened. I was seeing gray things flying around. They had wings and they were ugly. At a ladies' prayer meeting, I asked them to pray for me again. They asked me about my medicine bag and said I needed to get rid of it. It broke my heart and I sobbed uncontrollably. I said I would though. I went home and put the medicine bag in a file cabinet. No one would know, I thought to myself, and I at least got rid of the leather pouch around the bag. Things quieted down. Then, Dea

came to our church and spoke on deliverance. I had always felt that Native Americans and Christianity had a lot in common. I thought I should ask Dea about it, and defend my side of the story. After telling him what I felt, we began praying. While praying I began chanting and singing as if I were physically an Indian. I felt angry and wanted to fight, but Dea and the Lord were holding on. I heard this scream and realized it was me. Prayer was again offered over me, but more fervently this time. That scream came again and a ferocity of bellowing. After that was all over, I confessed to several of my dearest friends what I had done about the medicine bag. I went home and destroyed the medicine bag contents once and for all. I knew that there was nothing there that had any meaning to me. Thank You Jesus for loving me so much."

Physical objects can be a go-between for a demon and a believer. In the Old Testament, Israelites were warned:

> **"Nor shall you bring an abomination into your house. . .You shall utterly detest it and utterly abhor it, for it is an accursed thing"** (Deuteronomy 7:26).

In the New Testament, James wrote that believers should:

> **"abstain from things polluted by idols"** (Acts 15:20).

Notice he said abstain from **"things."** That could be food. . . or maybe a medicine bag? Just as demons can enter a life by their "touching" certain physical objects dedicated to Satan, so demons can be expelled in the same way by certain things dedicated to Christ.

> **"God worked unusual miracles by the hands of Paul, so that even handkerchiefs or aprons were brought from his body to the sick, and the diseases left them and the evil spirits went out of them"** (Acts 19:11).

Hallelujah! If the devil thinks a crystal ball is powerful, wait until he is confronted by your future anointed handkerchief!

Paul had doubtless warned the Ephesians about the occult. Many of them became believers as Acts 19:18 says:

> **"And many who had BELIEVED came** (Christians, not unbelievers!), **confessing and telling their deeds."** Or as the GW translation clarifies:

> **"Many believers openly admitted their involvement with magical spells and told all the details."**

Then Verse 19 shows the need to get rid of demonic objects, in this context, books:

> **"Also, many of those who had practiced magic brought their books together and burned them in the sight of all. And they counted up the value of them, and it totaled fifty thousand pieces of silver."**

Wow, 50,000! Their interest in the occult obviously went far beyond an astrological forecast in the newspaper! The deeper the interest, the deeper the bondage and the greater the need for true repentance, which includes a spiritual separation AND a physical separation from anything demonic. Paul considered false religion a form of witchcraft:

> **"O foolish Galatians! Who has bewitched you**
> **that you should not obey the truth"**
> (Galatians 3:1).

Fiddling with the occult will bring negative results, but it, of itself, is not a sin that will damn one to hell. However, fiddling with the truth of our salvation can be a "sin unto death."

> **"He who has the Son has life; he who does not**
> **have the Son of God does not have life. . .**
> **If anyone sees his brother sinning a sin which**
> **does not lead to death, he will ask, and He will**
> **give life for those who commit sin not leading**
> **to death"** (1 John 5:12, 16).

The deliverance ministry is not for sinners. The preaching of the gospel is! The deliverance ministry is for those who have already become believers and now "have life." They just need a brother or sister in Christ who knows how to pray, knows their authority over the devil, and can help them experience the "abundant life" of which John 10:10 speaks.

Demons who enter by witchcraft usually cause the most conspicuous and observable manifestations, probably because witchcraft is the most blatant invitation and door-opener to demons. I found, for instance, that the easiest way to pick up a "spirit of fear" is to dabble in the occult.

When I pastored in Fruitland, Idaho two women came to me for help. They were roommates. One of them said, "I can't take it anymore! You've got to talk to her!" She then left the room so I could counsel with her friend who proceeded to tell me of a great struggle with fear. She'd "sense" someone looking in her bedroom window at night and would flee to her roommate's bedroom.

I asked her if she had ever had anything to do with the occult. First, she said "no" but later remembered something strange that had happened years ago. She was visiting with some friends in a trailer and while they were sitting at the table talking, for no apparent reason, a bottle opener just shot suddenly across the room. A man at the table said, "Hey, it's a demon. Let's conjure it up!" They began reciting the Lord's Prayer, backward.

Without warning, the man started choking himself. I have had several people try to choke me while ministering deliverance. It's very unnerving to say the least. Because of my experiences, I could easily believe her story.

It so freaked her out that she fled the trailer. As she was running down the street, she turned and observed a black form following her. She admitted that ever since that time she had had the fear. I told her it was a demon, and I was going to cast it out. When I took authority over the spirit, she felt something lift from her. When she went home, she discovered that she was delivered!

If Americans only knew who they were dealing with when they find themselves fascinated with the occult, witchcraft, and false religions!

15

Trauma

"Deliver us from evil"
(Matthew 6:13 KJV).

Jesus taught us to pray in the Lord's Prayer, "Deliver us from evil." Many translations say, "Deliver us from the EVIL ONE." Any kind of evil opens the door to the evil one. One of these greatest evils is trauma.

Stronghold #4: Trauma

Trauma is another result of the fall of man and the work of the devil. Jesus revealed that one of His reasons for coming to earth was to deal with mankind's trauma.

> **"The Spirit of the Lord is upon me, because he hath anointed me to preach the gospel to the poor; he hath sent me to heal the brokenhearted, to preach deliverance to the captives, and recovering of sight to the blind, to set at liberty them that are bruised"** (Luke 4:18 KJV).

Jesus came to "heal the brokenhearted." The word for brokenhearted is a compound word from three Greek words meaning "broken in heart." The heart (Greek: cardia) represents our thoughts and feelings. The word "broken" (Greek: suntribo) means "crushed completely" or "broken to shivers."

Trauma is not like some black and blue bruise after being hit which hurts for a while but then completely heals and goes away. It is a hurt so deep that it never completely heals. Traumatized people have been completely crushed or broken apart inside. They are not whole, nor can they be until they are healed of these inner wounds. We call this healing "deliverance." We call these wounds "trauma."

The Definition of Trauma

1a: an injury (such as a wound) to living tissue caused by an extrinsic agent

b: a disordered psychic or behavioral state resulting from severe mental or emotional stress or physical injury

c: an emotional upset

2: an agent, force, or mechanism that causes trauma

Trauma is the Greek word for "wound". Although the Greeks used the term only for physical injuries, nowadays, trauma is just as likely to refer to emotional wounds. We now know that a traumatic event can leave psychological symptoms long after any physical injuries have healed. The psychological reaction to emotional

trauma now has an established name: post-traumatic stress disorder, or PTSD. It usually occurs after an extremely stressful event, such as wartime combat, a natural disaster, or sexual or physical abuse; its symptoms include depression, anxiety, flashbacks, and recurring nightmares. (End quote: Source: "Trauma." Merriam-Webster's Unabridged Dictionary, Merriam-Webster, https://unabridged.merriam-webster.com/unabridged/trauma. Accessed 8 May. 2021)

Indeed, there are physical, emotional, and mental wounds that can so traumatize a soul that only deliverance can bring lasting healing. Deaths, car accidents, abuses of all kinds, terrifying experiences, physical attacks, rape, and anything else that a psychiatrist might conclude was the origin of psychological problems can be the origin of demonic problems begun by trauma.

Sharing people's (anonymous) personal stories would be the best way to illustrate how trauma affects people. Consider the following testimonies we have received:

Post-Traumatic Stress Disorder

"The doctors diagnosed me as having Post-Traumatic Stress Disorder (PTSD), which has a lot of reference to panic attacks and immense fear for reasons that don't seem to be going on at the time. I walked in that for five years now. I was on different medications and different things that did not work well. I had been continuing in the power of the Lord, but never had deliverance. At the time we prayed, there was a real manifestation of fear I had. Certain people could enter the room, and I would want to run. It hasn't happened since. I had four chances the next day to test my deliverance and thank God I came home with a smile on my face and a dance in my heart. It is definite deliverance. I am not taking the medication now. The fear is gone!"

Loneliness, Hate, Suicide, Self-Mutilation

"I had loneliness, abandonment, hate, suicide, self-mutilation, bulimia, selfishness, torment, abuse, and depression. You prayed for me. I want you to know that God has delivered me. Since I was prayed for, God took His angels and covered my ears from the enemy. The enemy always waited until I left the church and would fill me with so much unbelief. But, since then, I have been able to eat and not throw up, nor feel the heaviness in my stomach or thoughts of vomiting. Praise God! And I have peace, calmness, and a positive feeling. I have also stopped doing self-mutilation. Thank you and thank God!"

Abandoned, Neglected, and Unloved

"By age 4, I had experienced severe trauma: incest, sexual molestation, physical, emotional, and mental abuse, living in a violent household. I saw my parents chasing each other with knives. My parents separated, and I was abandoned, physically and emotionally neglected, and unloved. I was not allowed to speak growing up. As an adult, I would frequently put my hand over my mouth as I spoke. There was a heaviness and acid eating away at me inside. There was trauma, rage, death, and silence. Through His servant Dea, God changed my life. I believe He has prepared me my whole life for these days. The Lord took away my childhood trauma, every violation, every act, everything that came against me. These are no longer a part of who I am. The heaviness lifted. I shared my testimony with my brother, and he accepted Christ as his Savior. Because of the freedom I received, I was able to speak of what in the past had to be silent. I have lungs again. I feel refreshed. Glory be to God."

Sexual Molestation and Murder

"My parents divorced before I was two. Mom remarried before I was three. My stepfather began sexually abusing me when I was six, and this continued about once or twice a week for four years. Mom divorced my stepfather and hooked up with another man. He also sexually abused me. When I was about thirteen years old, I told my two older brothers, aged fifteen and sixteen, what my stepfather had done to me. They went into a rage and killed him. They went to prison for it. I started to overeat and then purge myself, sometimes twice a day and sometimes not for a month (and never when pregnant with children!). I became a spirit-filled Christian and served God. I married and had four children. On July 10th, 1997, I came to church expecting to be set free. While in the prayer line, Dea asked me to whisper in his ear what the problem was. I had never told anyone, and my weak flesh almost gave in. I wanted to tell him something else, but the Lord told me to tell the truth. I did. When I was prayed for, I felt as if a load was lifted from my inside. I was filled with a spirit of encouragement and peace. I knew I was delivered and would never return and could walk and grow deeper with the Lord and be His servant. Thank you, Lord, for revival!"

The Death of a Dog

"I have known for many years that I had "issues" in my life, things that constantly tripped me up or kept me ineffective as a Christian. When I was five years old, I had a female dog named "Flicka." One day we went for a walk, and Flicka decided to stop in the neighbor's driveway and lie down. The neighbor lady backed up and ran over her, killing her. The whole thing horrified me. This was my first experience with death. Then my grandmother died. I began having nightmares. Sometimes I felt paralyzed with fear. I also began to see a being in my parents' bedroom. He was iridescent, shiny, and rainbow-like in color. His name was "Gring." Even though I was saved at the age of seventeen, nightmares continued. I was also overcome by an intense fear of death. I was always afraid that either I or someone I loved was going to die. These thoughts and dreams plagued me for twenty-seven years. The first night of the crusade, I told the Lord that I was tired of the bondage in my life and that I would do ANYTHING He asked me or told me to do to get free *(That's the problem with many; they aren't serious enough with God! Dea)*. God began to reveal things to me that had happened in my life, things I had forgotten about years ago. I began to repent of sins and renounce past involvement in sinful activities. I wasn't entirely delivered the first night, but the experience was exhausting. As Dea prayed and took authority over demonic strongholds in my life, I felt like I couldn't breathe. And then I felt so nauseous. After I went home, the Lord continued to reveal things in my life that had opened doors to demonic oppression. Nausea increased to the point of gagging. The following day, I had a vision which I believe revealed Gring's actual identity — a demon! I was prompted by the Lord to fast the entire day, and throughout the day I took authority over every demonic stronghold the Lord revealed to me. That night, Dea prayed with me again. This time I was completely set free! The only way to describe what I felt is to say that it was refreshing, like drinking an ice-cold glass of water on a hot day. Since then, I have not had any nightmares. The thought of death doesn't seem to have any effect on me. I praise God for what He has done in my life. HALLELUJAH!"

A Distrust of God

"I was saved and baptized with the Holy Spirit just before I turned twenty-one. Yet, there has always been distrust of God, and I could not receive the full love and life of God. While Dea and others of the church prayed for me, the Lord brought a step-uncle to my mind. We were supposed to go to the store, but on the way back, he took a detour. He then made advances toward me and said, 'That will teach you not to trust anybody.' I hadn't realized how much that affected my walk with God. I also saw at this time that many unclean spirits had come in and there were idols in my life. A spirit of spiritual death had not allowed me to receive the fullness of the love and life of God that I saw in His Word. I know God has delivered me, and I am now walking in freedom in these areas, receiving God's grace and His love."

A Home With a "Lot of Torment"

"When I was a little child, I grew up in a home where there was a lot of torment, alcoholism, drugs, fighting, sexual abuse, and beatings from my dad. My parents divorced. My mom had many boyfriends. One of them abused me sexually. I got pregnant at sixteen. My step-grandfather was very religious and went to church, but he abused me sexually. So that was my view of God, and I wanted nothing to do with God. When I was twenty-three, I met the Lord for the first time, yet my walk was a real struggle. From all the past, there was deep hurt and pain. For twenty years, I struggled to walk with God but could never give myself over to Him completely. I became overcome by a terrible fear. No one but God, and I know the turmoil that I had gone through for years. When Dea wanted to pray for people who had become overcome by desperate fear and torment, I knew that was me. The minute Dea touched me, I felt a hand or something go down deep and yank a tree out of me. It was incredible. I haven't been the same since. I have joy and peace. I am a new person."

As I reread these testimonies sent to me, I was reminded of how traumatic sexual abuse is. These testimonies were all from females, the primary object of the abuse of evil men.

One out of five women is sexually molested or raped.

The above testimonies bear witness that after such attacks, demonic bondage is usually the result! The answer is not counseling alone. The answer is casting out a demon! Luke 10:25-37 tells us the Good Samaritan story. Verse 30 says:

> **"A certain man went down from Jerusalem to Jericho, and fell among thieves, who stripped him of his clothing, wounded him, and departed, leaving him half dead** (now THIS was a traumatic experience!)."

Verse 34 adds that the Good Samaritan:

> **"went to him and bandaged his wounds** (Greek: trauma)"

Note that he "went to him." Most people don't realize the source of their hurts. They need someone to make the effort to assist them. Won't you?

We have a cure for wounded people who were traumatized as those people were you read about. It is the power of the Blood of the Lamb applied like a bandage to their wounded soul.

We know that the Lord is the Deliverer.

> **"He is the healer of the brokenhearted. He is the one who bandages their wounds"** (Psalm 147:3 GW).

Yet, we are His instruments to enforce His work on the Cross to:

> **"heal the brokenhearted...and to set at liberty them that are bruised"** (Luke 4:18 KJV).

Wounded people need Jesus' help. And they need a Good Samaritan. They need a deliverer! Want to help your brokenhearted and bruised neighbors? If so, Jesus said in verse 37 that you should follow the example of the Good Samaritan:

"GO and DO likewise."

Know anyone who has experienced trauma? Christ's command requires action:

"GO"…"DO!"

16

Curses

"the curse causeless shall not come"
(Proverbs 26:2 KJV).

An obvious corollary of the above Scripture is simply this:

"If someone is under a curse, it came upon them for a reason."

We want to study in this chapter what those reasons are and how to break off any curses. This is an important biblical study because the word "curse" is used over one-hundred times in the Bible, and the word "cursed" is used seventy-two times! This is no minor subject!

Stronghold # 5: Curses

We can understand more about the meaning of a curse from what Merriam-Webster says below. I will add a few brief comments in parenthesis:

curse *noun* \ *'kərs*

1a: a calling to a deity to visit evil on one:

(Someone telling another, "God _ _ _ _ you," is an example of this! We don't call it "cursing" for nothing!)

a solemn pronouncement or invoking of doom or great evil on one:

(We have all heard people say, "May God strike me dead!")

b: any utterance marked by malediction or execration: oath

(In Judges 11:29-40, Jephthah made an oath to sacrifice to God the first thing that came out of his house if He would help him win a battle. His daughter was the first one out! He cursed his own flesh and blood!)

c: evil effects brought about by a curse or by or as if by something cursed

<a witch putting a curse on them> <an ancient house and family on which a curse had long rested>

2: ex-communication or anathema: formal and extreme church censure

3: something that is cursed or worthy of being cursed: an evil, misfortune, or source of harm: scourge

4: menstruation

(Source: Merriam-Webster's Unabridged Dictionary, Merriam-Webster, https://unabridged.merriamwebster.com/unabridged/curse. Accessed 8 May. 2021)).

I almost deleted that 4th definition above, for obvious reasons, then I realized something significant. Menstruation was the first curse pronounced by God against woman for her sin in the Garden of Eden:

> **"Then he said to the woman, "I will sharpen the pain of your pregnancy, and in pain you will give birth"** (Genesis 3:16 NLT).

The first effect of this curse on Eve would have been that she menstruated before becoming pregnant. Later, "The Curse" became slang for a woman having her period.

The second curse was against man. I am looking out my office window as I write. I can see weeds sprung up among the blades of grass and in the flower beds. Weeds was the first curse God pronounced on Adam after the fall:

> **"Cursed is the ground for your sake. . .both thorns and thistles it shall bring forth for you"** (Genesis 3:17, 18).

Yes, God is behind some curses. One of the most critical curses He pronounced was against those who oppose Israel. In Genesis 12:2, 3, God told Abraham (the Father of the Israel Nation):

> **"I will make you a great nation. . . I will bless those who bless you, And I will curse him who curses you."**

How many of our blessings in America are because we have been such a loyal friend of Israel? May God have mercy on us if we ever turn our backs on the Jews!

Sin causes family curses (case in point, our progenitors, Adam and Eve!). God pronounced a family curse on sin in the Old Testament Law of God:

> **"Don't bow down to them** (idols) **and don't serve them because I am God, your God, and I'm a most jealous God, punishing the children for any sins their parents pass on to them to the third, and yes, even to the fourth generation of those who hate me"**
> (Exodus 20:5 MSG).

It is interesting that this generational curse was mentioned in the context of worshipping idols since we learned earlier that demons get involved in idol worship! The Authorized Version translates Exodus 20:5 using the following phrase:

> **"visiting the iniquities of the fathers upon the children."**

"Visit" or "visitation" is used many times in the Authorized Version of the Old Testament, speaking of God "coming down" and getting involved, personally seeing that things happen on earth. It was often a time of disastrous vengeance by God.

"Iniquities" are sins that are especially crooked or perverse. They become like roots, crookedly digging their way into the dirt, making a tree stand more permanently. Likewise, curses are roots that must be pulled out and then "cast out" (A demon) so that the tree (the life of the curse) will die.

Freemasonry (a source of occult bondage) has proven to be a deep root of curses on many families. Make sure this curse is broken in your life and in anybody else's life that you are working with to receive deliverance. Be sure to ask about family members, present or past, who are or were freemasons.

The Old Testament mentions curses often. Then curses continued into the New Testament. Jesus said that sinners who are hell-bound are cursed:

> **"Depart from Me, you cursed, into the everlasting fire prepared for the devil and his angels"** (Matthew 25:41).

Paul reiterated in Galatians 3:10 the truth of Deuteronomy 27:26 that those who break God's laws are cursed:

> **"it is written, 'Cursed is everyone who does not continue in all things which are written in the book of the law, to do them.'"**

Peter described those who:

> **"want to look for nothing but the chance to commit adultery; their appetite for sin is never satisfied. They lead weak people into a trap. Their hearts are trained to be greedy. They are under God's curse!"**
> (2 Peter 2:14 GNT).

Curses are real. God created some of them. But the devil and evil men also bring curses into existence, and it is these curses that I wish to primarily address in this chapter.

Demonic Curses

Satan lied to and tempted Eve. She yielded to that lie, and a curse resulted. The previous chapter was filled with testimonies of people who were under curses, curses that Satan had brought upon them, or curses that men had brought upon them. When patterns of repeated bad things happen to people, we should always suspect a curse. And where there is a curse, a demon won't be far behind.

A woman had been kidnapped and kept captive for a decade, until she was finally rescued. I just read this morning that some car-jackers pulled in front of that same woman, robbed her, and stole her car. She is surely living under a curse! I was sharing with my wife how our family has never experienced such horrible things. We are not living under a curse. We are living in a basket of blessing:

> **"The blessing of the Lord makes one rich, And He adds no sorrow with it"** (Proverbs 10:22).

Yet, thank God, there is deliverance from curses. Following is a testimony that demonstrates curses in action:

"I was the sixth of a family of eight children. We were raised by my mother because my father was in prison. My mom was raped by her father at a young age *(Thus birthing a family curse-Dea)*. She worked at bars and had a lot of boyfriends and four different husbands. We grew up on welfare. My oldest brother was raping my sister for years, and there were a lot of drugs. I think sexual abuse came into my life from my mother's boyfriends. I was real unruly and at twelve, had a boyfriend who was eighteen. He introduced me to drugs. I went from boyfriend to boyfriend, always older. One boyfriend introduced me to killing cats, bondage, explicit things like that. My mom gave him custody of me when I was sixteen. He would abuse me physically a lot. He went to prison for it. I went to college and then got involved with Hell's Angels. I got involved with more drugs. I met a man who led me to Christ. He was the first man I ever knew who didn't want me for sex. I was always used, maybe even passed around. But, he was different. We have now been married ten years. Yet, still, I never stayed on track with God. My husband told me there was an evangelist at the church that could cast out demons. So, I came to the church the next night prepared. I was harboring a lot of hate in me. I was going to scream and be sick. There was pain in my stomach and head. The demons came out, and I saw them; two of them looked like men who had abused me. One was laughing at me. It was like I was standing outside of my body watching. Then, it was like a clear blue tunnel, and it was real cool. When I got up this morning, I felt like Satan was laughing at me and saying, "Are you crazy?" So, I started singing in the Spirit!"

Did you catch that? She was "singing in the Spirit." This Spirit-filled Christian was still under a curse, though she had been saved and filled with the Holy Spirit.

Curses are caused by words or by actions. The law of sowing and reaping is always at work in those words and actions:

> **"Do not be deceived. . .** (curses begin by deceiving spirits or people who are deceived); **for whatever a man sows, that he will also reap. For he who sows to his flesh will of the flesh reap corruption"** (Galatians 6:9, 10).

The above word "flesh" describes things like abuse, sexual sins, drugs, and the actions of men, which lead to "corruption." You can see in the above testimonies how fleshly curses opened doors to demonic curses

How do we deal with curses? In the Old Testament, curses had to often be nullified by the shedding of people's blood. The shedding of blood is also necessary in the New Testament, but it is through the blood of one man:

> **"Christ has redeemed us from the curse of the law, having become a curse for us (for it is written, "Cursed is everyone who hangs on a tree"), that the blessing of Abraham might come upon the Gentiles in Christ Jesus, that we might receive the promise of the Spirit through faith"** (Galatians 3:13).

There were 691 commands given under the Old Testament Law that were impossible for fallen mankind to keep, thus all were subject to curses. In the New Testament, through Christ's work on the Cross, every curse can be broken!

A Witch's Curse?

So often, I have had people tell me that they think some witch has put a curse upon them. In America, this would probably be a relatively rare thing. In places like Jamaica or Africa, this might be true. Remember in chapter nine that my first personal experience with demons was while visiting "The Prayer Garden" where the missionary, Sister Gladys, pastored.

Sister Gladys was no novice when it came to dealing with demons. In Africa, she would serve as a midwife for women in childbirth. One time a baby was born with the umbilical cord wrapped around its neck. Sister Gladys unwrapped the cord, but then it snapped back around the throat again. She again unwound the cord, but then it rewound itself around the baby's neck once more.

The missionary knew she was dealing with witchcraft (the natives were steeped in it). She began to speak to the demons and commanded them to let go. Sister Gladys was able to break the curse and get the winding action stopped so that the baby was safely born. When is the last time you ever heard of such a thing in America?

Evangelist Kenneth Hagin told the story of the time someone warned him that a witch was going to put a curse on him. Brother Hagin told him to say to the witch, "I double-dog dare you!" He knew his authority in Christ and the truth that, "the curse causeless shall not come" (Proverbs 26:2 KJV).

How could a witch put a curse on you if you have given no cause for such a curse to fall on you? So, let's put aside our memories of all the curses put on Walt Disney princesses by witches and get down to business with the real problems we might be facing with curses.

The curse closest to home in my life is the curse of alcoholism. My dad was an alcoholic. He took his first drink at seven years of age. . . and loved it! As I was growing up, I didn't know from one day to the next if I would come home from school and find my dad drunk (he would later in life get delivered from alcoholism and became a pastor!). Thank God that demon didn't get a hold of me, but it did my older brother, Ed.

Ed was an alcoholic. He was a high-school counselor during the day, but when he came home at night, he would commonly drink a six-pack of beer and two shots of hard liquor. His wife became an alcoholic and died of advanced alcoholism in her fifties. My brother accepted Christ in his sixties and eventually quit drinking. Unfortunately, the damage had been done to his health, and he died with Alzheimer's.

My brother buried two wives, both who had died of alcoholism.

Ed's son, Shane, became an alcoholic. Like his dad, for years, he would hold a job down and then drink in the evenings or weekends. Eventually, booze got the best of him though. He lost his job and family and ended up living on the streets for years. In his fifties, he was found dead, surrounded by bottles of liquor.

Shane's son became an alcoholic too and has been in and out of treatment centers.

Would anybody reading this doubt for a moment that alcoholism was a curse in my family? It is just the grace of God that I somehow circumvented that curse! Following is someone who was not able to evade the curse in her family:

> "I have been a Christian for a long time, but I still was suffering from panic disorder, anxiety, and obsessive-compulsive disorder (OCD). I knew that these were things that came from my past. My great-grandmother was a high covenant witch in the occult. My mother also practiced witchcraft. . .

(Let me interject here: the curse did not come because relatives who were witches on purpose put a curse on her. Loving family members wouldn't do that! But their involvement in witchcraft in itself resulted in generational curses falling upon her!)

. . .I was on medication for the OCD. I would have rapid heartbeat. I always counted to number seven, so nothing bad would happen to me. I would click lights off and on seven times. I am a nurse, so in my field, I dealt with many personalities with disorders like me. I was afraid a lot. I was afraid at night. I was afraid of death. If I had pain, I thought it was cancer. I remember as a young child when that demon came on me. I was only six, but I felt depressed from that day on. I knew that I would die any day. The night you prayed for me, I started to feel nauseated and felt like something was being birthed through my mouth. It was the strangest feeling. I started to get sick and started to vomit, but there wasn't anything there. Yet, I felt like things were coming out of me. Every time a word would come to my head, such as loneliness, fear, death, panic, or lust, I knew that those actually were spirits that had hung on me for a long time. It has been three days now, and I don't count or recount anymore. I also was delivered from a strange pain in my side. I am not worried about medication anymore. The Lord has given me a sense of honesty and cleanliness inside. It is freedom. I feel like a brand-new person."

Children come under curses, and when they grow into adulthood, the curses are still there. Such curses call for the deliverance ministry! The above woman was educated. She was a Christian. You can be sure that she prayed frequently through the years about her problems and counseled with others. She fought long and hard to overcome these terrible bondages.

Then one day, out of perhaps thirty years (Over 10,000 days) of living, she found her answer. She wasn't free until that one day when someone who knew how to cast out demons came her way.

Don't you long to be able to help people like her? In the next chapter, we will learn how to cast out demons and break curses.

Thank God that in the coming Kingdom of God:

> **"No longer will there be a curse upon anything"** (Revelation 22:3 NLT).

But until then, the world needs the deliverance ministry!

17

How to Cast Out Demons
(Part 1)

**"But if I cast out demons with the finger of
God, surely the kingdom of God has
come upon you"** (Luke 11:20).

"The finger of God" phrase which Jesus used in the above
verse would have reminded the Israelites of Exodus 8:19:

"This is the finger of God."

This was what the Egyptian magicians said to Pharaoh after
they couldn't replicate the curse of lice covering Egypt. What is
the finger of God? Rightly dividing the Word, we know exactly
what it is. Jesus said in Matthew 12:28:

"I cast out demons by the Spirit of God."

Moses "cast" the Israelites out of Egyptian bondage by "the
finger of God" which was the manifestation of the power of the
Spirit of God. We cast demons out of people in bondage also
by the Holy Spirit's power. If you want to be used of God in
deliverance, you need to learn to cooperate with the Holy Spirit.

In Luke 11:21, 22, Jesus continues talking about deliverance:

> **"When a strong man, fully armed, guards his own palace, his goods are in peace. But when a stronger than he comes upon him and overcomes him, he takes from him all his armor in which he trusted, and divides his spoils."'**

We know that Jesus is referring to spiritual warfare in the above verses because he adds in Verse 24:

> **"When an unclean spirit goes out of a man. . ."**

If Jesus needed the help of the Holy Spirit to cast out demons, then how much more do you and I need the Spirit's help! The deliverance ministry requires a deep reliance upon the Holy Spirit's assistance:

> **"For as many as are led by the Spirit of God, these are sons of God"** (Romans 8:14).

Pray for the Spirit's guidance. Pray for His daily infilling. Pray in the Spirit often. Expect the Spirit to lead you to people who need deliverance and then to assist you as "the finger of God" pointing out the hidden presence of demons.

When I first started to read books seeking to understand more about the deliverance ministry, I discovered that varying ministries took somewhat different approaches. What is the "official" way to cast out demons?

There is NO one official method!

There is more than one way to skin a cat. There are different approaches surgeons take, depending on their training, the diagnosis, and the health of the patient. I have often said that I believe you could put a new convert in a room with a Bible and someone with a demon and if they would just do what they read in the Word and stick with it, they could eventually get that demon out.

Nevertheless, some methods have proven to be more effective than others. In this chapter I will primarily suggest the approach and techniques that I have used for many years. It may not be the best method, but it has worked in many churches. At the end of chapter 20, I will refer you to some other books (by men wiser than I!) that you could study if you are interested in learning more about this important subject. Below are steps I recommend you take:

Detection

"If it looks like a duck, swims like a duck, and quacks like a duck, then it probably is a duck!"

How can we know for sure if it is a duck, uh, I mean a demon? The most obvious and biblical way to know if someone has a demon is through the gift of "discerning of spirits" (See 1 Corinthians 11:10). As of this writing, I do not have the gift of "discerning of spirits," though I pray for it every day! I am quite sure it may operate from time to time, or it could be the gift of the word of knowledge which does operate at times in my life.

You don't need a special gift if you will do what I do. I primarily use the natural gift of "detection." If something comes to my mind when I am ministering (fear, rejection, lust, etc.), I am not sure if it is by the Holy Spirit or simply experience, but I will take time to speak words against that.

I was preaching in a church (where I had advertised a ministry of deliverance) and confessed from the pulpit that I didn't have the gift of discerning of spirits. One woman in the congregation gasped loudly, as though to say:

> **"How dare you claim to have a deliverance ministry but don't have the gift of discerning of spirits!"**

Well, the primary purpose of this book is to convince people who normally sit in the pews and don't claim to have any special gifts that they can still be used of God. You can heal the sick without the "gift of healing" (refer to chapters 1-8), and you can cast out demons without some special anointing or spiritual gift. It is not the spiritual gifts that cast out demons; remember, it is the Person of the Holy Spirit! Join me in praying that God will grant you and me both the privilege of the gift of discerning of spirits.

If you do happen to have the gift, you will either see demons (I never have) or know by the Spirit they are there. Your gift will surface. You will know you have the gift. And others will acknowledge that gift in you.

Wise pastor, if you discover someone in your congregation has this gift, take advantage of their gift often. Encourage them to inform you if they discern an evil spirit. Release them to be a blessing at altar calls by helping you pray with people. Sanction your women's and other small group leaders to fully utilize their gift which works especially well in smaller group gatherings anyway.

If you have the gift, don't walk up to somebody and say, "The Lord shows me you have a demon!" Instead, be "wise as serpents and harmless as doves" (Matthew 10:16).

"A servant of the Lord. . .must be kind to everyone, be able to teach, and be patient with difficult people" (2 Timothy 2:24 NLT).

Demonized people can be "difficult people" indeed! When you detect a demon, I suggest you (with a big smile on your face!) unpretentiously, and quietly, say something like: "Is there something in your life you are struggling with and feel you need the Lord's help to overcome? I would love to pray with you about it."

Never pressure people to get delivered. I have found that there is often a work of the Spirit in one's life that must be accomplished before they are ready to obtain freedom.

If you don't have the gift of discerning of spirits yet, you can still use old-fashioned detection! A detective observes, asks questions, uses his best judgment, and arrests if he determines guilt. Be a detective for the Lord; observe, ask questions, and use your best judgment. The Lord will help you (and the person in need) to determine any demonic guilt so you can make an arrest!

If you detect unhappiness, fear, or depression, I have found that these are the most common denominators of folks with a demon. I have scanned the congregation seated on the platform and knew just by observation that a person or two likely had demons (which they usually proved to have!).

If someone admits their problem to you (because they already "detected" in themselves that there is something undoubtedly wrong in their life), then you can take it from there. When they or you are unsure, you can ask pointed (the finger of God) questions, while carefully showing love and compassion, "speaking the truth in love" (Ephesians 4:15).

Confession

"Confess your trespasses to one another, and pray for one another, that you may be healed" (James 5:16).

Ananias and Sapphira both lied to Peter, and not only were they not delivered from a lying spirit they died for it (Acts 5:1-11)! As a deliverance evangelist, I am dependent upon a Christian's willingness to be upfront and honest about their problem. If they are not ready to be honest, they are not ready to be delivered (This is an important aspect of repentance).

When I minister in a church, I often announce something like this at the altar call:

"If you are tormented with fear, depression, unforgiveness, were sexually molested, have deep emotional wounds, or experienced trauma in the past, God has given me a deliverance ministry. Please come forward and just whisper in my ear the problem and I won't embarrass you. I will pray for the Lord to set you free."

If they sneak out the back door instead of coming forward, either they don't want to be free or they aren't yet ready to be free (not repentant, not submitted enough to the Lord, couldn't keep themselves free after being set free). Even the best Psychiatrist can't help someone if they don't honestly share their problem. "Confess your trespasses" (as James 5:16

instructs us to do) is then a powerful biblical starting place for the process of deliverance.

Sometimes someone will have to confess something very graphic sexually. (The flesh enjoys hearing such things; Hollywood definitely takes advantage of prurient interests in most of their productions!). For this, and other obvious reasons, ideally, women will minister to women and men with men.

As a pastor of a small church and later as an evangelist who speaks in smaller churches, and usually travels without his wife, I have had to minister deliverance to hundreds of women, frequently by myself. I often ask the pastor's wife or a woman or two of faith to help me pray. Knowing that this would be my ministry, the Lord had to deal severely with areas of uncleanness in my life and I had to go through a long, deep, spiritual healing, and cleansing.

I have sat down for deliverance with more than one deliverance specialist (I want to make sure that I don't have any demons!). The last time I submitted myself for any necessary cleansing, a very seasoned warrior, author, and pastor kept praying over me and reporting, "You're clean. . .you're clean!"

Oh, those words were so encouraging! But they hadn't always been true of me as a Christian and even as a minister of the gospel. It didn't come without paying a price and taking a lot of spiritual baths through the years!

Let me forewarn you, if you get serious about delivering people from sins and demons, the Lord will require you to deal with your own sins and demons. It's the splinter and log in the eye principle (Matthew 7:4, 5)!

I am free from pornography. I have not stepped out on my wife in 50 years of marriage (as of June 25, 2021). God alone deserves the glory for that! I joyfully consider myself a father-in-the-faith (really more like a grandfather-in-the-faith now!) to both men and women.

Through God's work in me, I can handle anything women tell me (deliverers must be able to do so). You might be shocked at some of things women have had to admit, as you read about in earlier chapters! My testimony is the same as Paul the Apostle:

> **"And I thank Christ Jesus our Lord who has enabled me, because He counted me faithful, putting me into the ministry"** (1 Timothy 1:12).

I will often tell women who are showing a reticence to share intimate details from their life that they could not tell me anything that I haven't already heard. And I let them know that it isn't necessary to know the details anyway. A simple, "I was molested as a child" or, "I was raped by my boyfriend," is usually all you'll need to know to get a demon of lust out, for instance.

Beware of the tricks of the trade of demons! Some people are afraid of demons:

> **I am far more afraid of my wife than I am of demons!**

Trust me, the last thing you need to be afraid of is a demon! Fear of a counterattack from hell, for example, is another "device" of the devil. A pastor and his wife called me on the phone with two extensions. They were dealing with someone they suspected had a demon and wanted to know how to cast it out. I gave them some advice.

The worried wife said, "Yeah, but I've heard if you cast a demon out of someone, that demon may come back and attack you!" I said, "If you aren't a threat to the powers of darkness, what are you doing in the ministry!"

Christians were never intended to be huddled safely behind four walls singing, "Onward Christian Soldiers." We are called to be warriors, carrying the sword of the Spirit, the shield of faith, and the Name of Jesus, ever wreaking havoc among demons. We don't have time for fear.

The unsaved might love horror movies, frozen in awe and fear of demons. Me? I neither respect nor fear demons. You shouldn't either. May every believer fearlessly declare war on the kingdom of darkness!

The devil is a master at using fear. We had a Satan worshipper come to a church I pastored. Some of the members were joining me in ministering deliverance. It took several of us to hold him down while others waged warfare. A 12-year-old boy was experiencing his first demonic manifestation. It was thrilling to him.

He wanted to get in on the action. During a brief lull in the "Come outs!" he boldly stepped forward and said, "I command you to come out of him!" The Satanist lifted his head, stared at the boy and with an angry, evil grimace said, "I'm going to kill you kid!"

I wish you could have seen the color go out of the boy's face as he quickly changed from bold warrior to scaredy cat. It was funny to me, as I knew after many deliverance sessions how a demon will try to scare you into leaving him alone (of course, that lying devil didn't and couldn't kill that kid!).

Demons lie! That shouldn't come as a surprise since the devil:

"is a liar and the father of it" (John 8:44).

A preacher uncle of mine believed my grandmother, who was in a rest home, had a demon and commanded it to come out. The demon spoke through his mom and said, "I'm not coming out and you can't make me come out!" My uncle believed the demon's lie and let it stay in her! Demons use fear and lies to avoid an exorcism. Be ready for this.

Concerning confession, the wisdom of an honest confrontation and renunciation of evil has been demonstrated repeatedly at Alcoholics Anonymous meetings. Those struggling with alcohol are encouraged to stand to their feet and confess, "I am an alcoholic." In their 12-Step Program, the 4th step is to have:

"Admitted to God, to ourselves, and to another human being the exact nature of our wrongs."

When you are satisfied that a candidate for deliverance is repentant, honest about his problems, and willing to "confess his trespasses," you are ready to move on to the next step.

Classification

Some deliverance ministers command demons to speak their name because they are convinced that it is necessary to know a demon's name to get it out. Such knowledge can help in getting a demon out more quickly. However, there is only one time in the Bible that any deliverance minister asked a demon its name: that is when Jesus asked for a name and the demon said:

"My name is Legion; for we are many"
(Mark 5:9, see also Luke 8:30).

There is no other example in the New Testament where anyone ever asked a demon for its name, so I don't think scripturally we can make this a hard and fast rule. I have tried this method and have not had much success with it.

One time I asked a demon its name and it said, "We are Legion!" I worked with that name for a while, commanding "Legion" to come out. When I wasn't getting a breakthrough, I asked again, "What is your name?" It said, "We are one!" I scratched my head and stopped asking that question and just kept commanding the demon to come out until it did.

At times when ministering deliverance, the person I was praying for knew the name of the demon and told me and I then used that name to cast it out. Identifying a demon by name helped me one time find my own freedom.

Let me (Dea) share my story:

I struggled with being a quitter. I would get excited and motivated on a project and then fizzle out on it. I would start new disciplines, like prayer or Bible reading, and get discouraged and give up. I would walk victoriously in some area of my life and then backslide to just like I was before. I could share more, but let me say, I needed deliverance! Then, one night, I woke up from a dream.

In the dream, I was wrestling with a demon. I understood, in the dream, that this was "the strong man," the demon I had been dealing with much of my life. The Lord even revealed to me his name in the dream. It was "Magamba" (I told this story in a church where there were some people from Nigeria who began to laugh upon hearing that name. They explained that the Nigerian word used to describe children who were out of control was magamba!).

Yes, in my childhood, Magamba entered my life and still affected me as an adult leader. After that dream, I knew with what I was dealing. I began to wage warfare and commanded Magamba, by name, to leave! I don't know if that demon was in me, on me, or around me; all I know is that God helped me develop a disciplined life. I have lifted weights faithfully for about two decades. The book you are now reading is my second, in just one year. It was a job, let me tell you! But, hallelujah, Magamba couldn't stop my forward progress (Oh, and I haven't had a sugary candy bar, sugary cookie, or sugary ice cream in over a year!).

I am grateful to the Lord for revealing to me a specific name of a specific demon I was dealing with. So, please understand, I am not against the discovery of a demon's name. It might help, as it did me. One thing I do know, however, you do not HAVE to know the name of every demon to cast them out. I have cast too many demons out WITHOUT knowing their name.

Besides that, if you ask a demon his name, you have begun a conversation. Those conversations, I learned in my earlier experiences, can go on and on and (at least to me) usually led nowhere. I prefer to just tell them to, "Be quiet!" That is, after all, exactly what Jesus told a talking demon in a synagogue:

"Be quiet, and come out of him!" (Mark 1:25).

Early on, I found it exciting and entertaining to spend time dealing with and talking with demons. Now, I prefer to just get them out as quickly as possible (so I can go get something to eat!). I like the way one person expressed it:

"If I want to talk to a demon, I'll write a note and tack it to the bottom of my shoe!" (see Romans 16:20).

I have my practice that I have continued for decades. Nevertheless, I must humbly acknowledge that many other deliverance ministries use methods, which differ from mine, that have worked equally well (or better!) for them.

My friend, whom I consider one of the greatest deliverance ministers in America, Dr. Douglas Carr, will at times talk to demons and ask them what right they have to be in a person. He reports that they are "proud" and usually answer such questions. If he thinks the demons are lying (which of course they can), Dr. Carr will ask the Holy Spirit to force the demon to tell the truth. He says that works really well. (You can order Dr. Doug Carr's book to learn his methods. The information to order it is at the end of the next chapter).

Read this book, hear my experiences, read the writings of other deliverance ministers, then: Choose your own weapons!

Though you may not need to know the name, it does help to know the type, category or classification of a demon or demons with which you are dealing. There are different types of demons, just as there are different types of people. Understanding this will help you in ministering deliverance. The Bible mentions:

- **"the spirit of jealousy"** (Numbers 5:30).

- **"the spirit of heaviness"** (Isaiah 61:3).

- **"a lying spirit"** (1 Kings 22:23).

- **"a spirit of infirmity"** (Luke 13:11).

- **"a familiar spirit"** (1 Samuel 28:7).

- **"a spirit of divination"** (Acts 16:16).

- **"the spirit of bondage"** (Romans 8:15).

Why didn't the Bible simply refer to them all as "evil spirits?" Probably for the same reason we don't call every male just a "man." Instead, we may call them names such as, "a thief, a liar, a murderer, mean, nice, good," etc. Demons, like people, are living beings. They have personalities. They have a certain character.

If the Holy Spirit took the effort to call out the classification of a demon, doesn't it seem that we should also? Even if the gift of discerning of spirits isn't operating, you will usually know what classification a demon is by how it manifests itself in a life.

Following is a partial list of what demons you might be confronting (alphabetically arranged and listing sub-categories. Some words fit in other categories as well).

Abuse: child abuse, sexual abuse, rape, abandonment, violence

Anger: wrath

Anxiety: worry, panic attacks

Bondage: could include everything from O.C.D. to sexual, or drug addictions, slavery to bad or unwanted habits, bulimia, anorexia, gluttony, (kind of an all-inclusive word in deliverance)

Condemnation: guilt, shame, feelings of unworthiness

Criticism: gossip, negativity

Depression: Chronic, over a long period of time (If you lost your job this past week, you are probably depressed about it, but you don't have a demon!)

Fear: fear of man, fear of the dark, fear of death, fear of the future, fear of rejection, phobias (unreasonable fears) of all kinds. There are about 100 classes of them!

Haunting: (refer to Chapter 19)

Imaginations: lust, fantasy, murderous thoughts

Infirmity: when doctors can't figure out what is wrong, or pains change locations, this could indicate a demon

Lust:

Lying:

Pride:

Rebellion: can't submit to authority, stubbornness

Rejection: self-hatred, abandonment

Religious spirit: spirit of legalism, spiritual pride, Freemasonry, Transcendental Meditation, and all false religions

Self-pity:

Sexual: fornication, adultery, masturbation, pornography, homosexuality, frigidity (often because of sexual molestation or rape), sexual perversions of any kind, even within the marriage bed.

Sorrow: loneliness, unable to get over the loss of a loved one, depression, unhappiness, sadness

Suicide:

Trauma: all types: physical, mental and emotional (refer to chapter 15)

Unforgiveness: resentment, bitterness, hatred, revenge (refer to chapter 14)

Witchcraft: anything to do with the occult, including, but not limited to, Astrology, Ouiji Board, Tarot Card Readings, ESP, Mind-Reading, Palm Reading, Seances, Autoprojection (out-of-the-body experiences), Telekinesis (moving objects with the mind), Voodoo (putting curses on people), Santeria, Fortune-telling, Satan worship (refer to chapter 14)

Quite a list, isn't it? Don't be overwhelmed by it. However, assume that if a Christian is unhappy, and living an unholy life, you have a justified reason to suspect any of the above.

Patiently work with the oppressed soul until they are completely free from any and all of these torments. Why? We can learn from the Lord's warning to Israel in Numbers 33:5 (GW):

> **"But if you do not force out those who live in the land, they will be like splinters in your eyes and thorns in your sides. They will constantly fight with you over the land you live in."**

Look closely: "Force out those (plural!) who live in the land." If you don't, "They will constantly fight with you over the land (body they) live in."

You can't see them, but I guarantee you they are there! If so, how do you get all these rascals out! We show you how, step by step, in the next chapter.

Stay awake for a little longer. . .

18

How to Cast out Demons
(Part 2)

"Behold, I cast out demons"
(Luke 13:32).

In Mark 1:23, 24 we learn an interesting fact:

> **"Now there was a man in their synagogue
> with an unclean spirit. And he cried out,
> saying, "Let us alone! What have we to do
> with You, Jesus of Nazareth? Did You come
> to destroy us? I know who You are--the Holy
> One of God!"**

First, notice that it says the man had "an unclean spirit" (singular), yet, the demon said, "Let us (plural) alone. . .Did You come to destroy us (plural)?" One demon was speaking for no telling how many others. We learn some important things from this verse:

1. One demon (apparently the leader or the "strong man" that Jesus spoke of in Mark 3:27) can do the talking for any other demons in a person.

2. When the Word says someone has "a demon" that doesn't mean there is only one.

3. It is often not enough to cast out one spirit. Be prepared to work on getting other hidden spirits out also.

4. Thus knowing each class of demon and working one by one on these until you get to the head honcho, so to speak, is pretty much the universally accepted method of deliverance.

A woman once came to me for deliverance and explained that the Lord had told her to:

"Make sure you get them all out."

I believe the Lord would tell us all to do the same! If there are several people praying over a tormented person, let one person take the lead, speaking to the demon (Perhaps the pastor, the most experienced, or other leaders). The others can just quietly pray and agree in faith. Yet, encourage everyone that if they "get anything" in their spirit (a name, a category, a trauma, etc.), to share with the leader and then he/she can approach the candidate for deliverance with this information.

> **"Two are better than one; because they have a good reward for their labor. For if they fall, the one will lift up his fellow. . .And if one prevail against him, two shall withstand him; and a threefold cord is not quickly broken"** (Ecclesiastes 4:9-12 KJV).

Praying in the Spirit

The Word does not specifically say that praying in the Spirit is a tool in casting out demons. One deliverance specialist said to me, "It stirs them up, but it won't cast them out." If you do pray in the Spirit, do it with the understanding that you are seeking the Holy Spirit's help in determining why a demon won't come out. That demonic control may be a mystery to you, but it certainly isn't to the Holy Spirit. (1 Corinthians 14:2):

> **"For he who speaks in a tongue. . .in the spirit he speaks mysteries"**

You read the testimony about the woman who had a spirit of fear because of praying the Lord's Prayer backward, seeking to conjure up a spirit. At first, she couldn't think of anything she had done that might have opened the door to her bondage to fear.

She was a Spirit-filled Christian, so I said, "Let's pray in tongues together for a while." We hadn't done that very long when she stopped me and said, "Oh, now I remember," and began recounting the story (you can reread it in Chapter 14).

From Jean S. from Ohio comes the following testimony:

> "You prayed for me Saturday evening. I did not feel or experience anything at that time. On Tuesday morning, I was driving to work (a twenty-minute drive). I decided I was going to pray in tongues all the way to work. I kept at it and began to get this sick feeling coming up out of my stomach, moving into my chest, and then it came out of my mouth as coughing and weird, strange noises. I continued praying in tongues, and about four or five times, this continued coming up out of my stomach. Finally, I stopped praying in tongues long enough to say, "In the name of Jesus, come out!" When this finally

stopped, I asked God if it was all out. I felt it was. I thank God for whatever that deliverance was."

Notice above that praying in the Spirit helped, but it wasn't until she actually commanded the demon to leave that it did! Believe me when I say: there are many Spirit-filled Christians out there that seek to live a holy life, seek to walk with the Holy Spirit, but are still bound up in an area of their life. Why? Because no one commanded the demon to leave yet! You can do that for them!

Notice also that she delivered herself. You have already read testimonies of people who were at home, alone, able to cast their demons out.

I was ministering in a church in California. A woman came for deliverance who had been involved in the occult. We cast the occult spirit out, and afterward, she raised her hands, joyfully exclaiming, "Free! Free! Free!" (Surely God had done a great work!) However, I felt she likely had other spirits still hiding and said, "Let's pray again and make sure you are completely free!" As we started to pray, sure enough, more demons began to manifest.

Many deliverance ministers feel that you need to discover who the leader of the pack over the other demons is. It is logical that the last demon to leave would be the strongest anyway.

Prayer and Fasting

You read the testimonies earlier of a few who felt led to fast the day they were believing for their deliverance. Virtually every deliverance minister that I know or read about used the discipline of fasting. Even Jesus didn't cast His first demon out until after fasting forty days.

Daniel fasted pleasant food for twenty-one days. It was revealed to him by the end of the fast that during all that time, spiritual warfare was taking place in the heavenlies (Daniel Chapter 10).

When the disciples couldn't cast a demon out of a tormented boy, they afterward asked Jesus why they couldn't cast it out. Jesus disclosed in Matthew 17:21:

"This kind does not go out except by prayer and fasting."

"This kind" shows that there is at least one class of demon that will not come out until somebody fasts. In this case, a suicidal demon who had so much control over the boy that he would cast him into a fire. Jesus had fasted, and they obeyed His command. The disciples hadn't yet fasted (but they would later). In Matthew 9:15, Jesus said that after He was gone, "Then they shall fast." So, disciple of Jesus, when are you fasting?

One time as my wife and I were casting out a demon, it spoke to us saying, "We are the kind that only comes out by prayer and fasting." That was the cleverest thing I ever heard a demon say! But even if he wasn't lying, thank God, I had already been living a fasting life for many years. (More about this subject in a later chapter).

One Proven Method of Deliverance

Make the candidate for deliverance comfortable. It is best not to leave them standing, as a demon might soon knock them to the floor anyway. If they are lying on the floor, have them sit in a pew or chair. (It is much easier to ask questions and make commands if you don't have to bend over or crouch over someone).

Let me interject: the person you are praying for does not have to have faith to be delivered. All the faith that is needed is yours!

1. Make sure there is no unforgiveness:

A man once approached at the altar of prayer and told me, "Every time I try to lift my hands to worship the Lord, my hands do like this (and he curled his fingers up, like in two claws, to show me)." I asked him if he had any unforgiveness in his life.

He said he did and told the story of how when he married his wife, his mother-in-law told him, "You just married her for sex." He had been bitter toward her ever since. I explained how to forgive, and he did. Then, I cast a spirit of unforgiveness out of him. Immediately, he could praise the Lord with extended fingers (and no manifestation of a demonic-like claw!).

So, when dealing with a person, I will usually ask, "Is there anybody in your past or your present that really hurt you, and you still feel anger, hatred, or unforgiveness toward them?" If they say they can't think of anyone, leave it there for the time being. If later, you don't feel you are making enough progress, revisit this subject.

If they admit to you that there is someone, explain to them that to be free, they must forgive everyone who has hurt them:

> **"But if you do not forgive men their trespasses, neither will your Father forgive your trespasses"** (Matthew 6:15).

> **"If you refuse to do your part, you cut yourself off from God's part"** (Matthew 6:15 MSG).

Share with them something along the lines of the following:

> "Forgiveness is not an emotion or a feeling. Forgiveness is a decision, an act of the will. God loved the world, so he made a decision to forgive mankind. He sent His Son to earth, choosing to not only forgive, but to also forget the sins of any who would repent and believe (Hebrews 10:17). To forgive anyone, you, like God, must make a decision to forgive.

> "God gave you a free will, and that will is the tool with which you forgive others. When you choose to forgive a person, make a statement of that forgiveness with your mouth. Then, like your Heavenly Father, let that settle it once and for all.

> "Forgiveness is not something you attempt to do, or work on for a while. There was a specific day that Christ came to earth to bring us salvation, December 25 or whenever. You can make today (i.e., June 27, 2021) the once and for all official day you forgave one and all.

> "You may not feel forgiveness yet, but you can mean it. Once the enemy is gone, you will feel better towards any you have had difficulty forgiving."

Next, demonstrate for them how to do this. Have them follow you along: *"Out loud (but not loud), say: 'Father, I forgive (tell them to say the name) for what they did. Forgive me for harboring unforgiveness."*

Ask them if there is anybody else. If so, have them do the same with the next person. I usually tell them to close their eyes and explain that they may see a face or have a memory of someone from their past. If they can't remember a name (or never knew it), they still need to say, "I forgive that person."

Afterward, prepare them by pointing out that the devil will likely come back and whisper in their ear: "Remember what he or she did to you!" You just tell him: "No, I refuse to take back your bondage. I have forgiven everyone."

When you (and the person) are convinced that everyone has been "officially" forgiven, you are ready for the next step.

2. Make sure they have renounced past involvement in witchcraft, the occult, or false religions AND Freemasonry:

Ask them if they have ever been involved in anything that had to do with the occult, witchcraft, religious cults, astrology, palm reading, tarot cards, Ouija board, seances, or other such things.

Often, they will say something like, "No...oh, I just remembered; one time, I did have my palm read." No matter how innocent their involvement in the occult might have been, just to make sure, have them follow you by sharing:

"2 Corinthians 4:2 says:

"We have renounced the hidden things. . ."

"You need to renounce past involvement in the occult. Before the Lord, recount everything you can think of that you ever did, that is related to hidden, secretive attempts to know things apart from the Word of God or through Jesus. So, say, 'Father, I renounce palm reading.' And then keep saying, "I renounce and continue naming everything that comes to your memory."

After you are satisfied they have successfully done this, you are ready for the next step.

3. Ask them if they have experienced trauma in their past.

I was praying for a woman in Oregon who, as I prayed, cried out, "It hurts!" I asked her, "What hurts?" She was taken back in her memory to when she was a child. She had received a terrible burn. When the nurses would come to her hospital bed to apply the ointments, the pain was traumatizing! It hurt! That physical and emotional trauma had stayed with her for a lifetime. She needed deliverance!

If your candidate for deliverance hasn't already shared past traumatic experiences, you first want to explain what you mean by "trauma" and give some common causes of PTSD (which we know can give place to a demon!). Quote some of the descriptions of trauma, which I recap from chapter 15:

> Trauma is the Greek word for "wound." Although the Greeks used the term only for physical injuries, nowadays, trauma is just as likely to refer to emotional wounds. We now know that a traumatic event can leave psychological symptoms long after any physical injuries have healed. The psychological reaction to emotional trauma now has an established name: post-traumatic stress disorder, or PTSD. It usually occurs after an extremely stressful event, such as wartime combat, a natural disaster, or sexual or physical abuse; its symptoms include depression, anxiety, flashbacks, and recurring nightmares.

(End quote: Source: "Trauma." Merriam-Webster's Unabridged Dictionary, Merriam-Webster, https://unabridged.merriam-webster. com/unabridged/trauma. Accessed 8 May. 2021)

More simply, you could ask:

"What do you feel is the most traumatic experience in your life; something, that if you were counseling with a psychiatrist, he would probably point to that ordeal as the root of your struggles?"

They almost always know what that incident was! After they share it, begin to take authority over it with a prayer something like this:

"I take authority over this trauma. I command every satanic power that used that event as an entry point to keep the person in bondage to COME OUT! Lord, we speak your promise in Psalm 147:3: "He heals the brokenhearted And binds up their wounds." Heal this broken heart. Bind up the wounds." If demons manifest, continue to pray.

In a sense, every demonic bondage results from a wound: self-inflicted, forced upon them by others, accidents, or tragedies. Make sure you spend ample time dealing with trauma. If you can't figure it out, take authority over it anyway!

A pastor once brought his daughter, maybe seven years old, into the prayer line. He reported that he and his wife had to leave a light on in her room because she was too afraid to sleep without it. I cast out that spirit of fear! The pastor later reported that his daughter hollered out at night from her bedroom, "Turn this light off. I can't fall asleep with it on!" Hallelujah, that's what I'm talking about!

4. Ask them if there is any major sin in their life of which they haven't yet fully repented.

We all have sins against which we struggle. That doesn't mean we have a demon. Nevertheless, some sins are not only the sinful nature or the flesh but have roots of demonic power. Better safe than sorry! But please, don't pry too much.

As you read in many testimonies, Christians had much more success over sin once demons were gone. And you don't want to minister condemnation to those who are already under a steady barrage of guilt from "the accuser of the brethren" (Revelation 12:10).

Usually, I won't even bring up the subject of sin (except the sin of unforgiveness and witchcraft), unless they mention it, it is revealed to someone helping me pray, or I am not seeing the relief I know, by experience, that they should have by now. (Remember the lady who was sleeping with men while her husband was away at war?) When she wasn't finding freedom, I asked her about sin. She confessed to adultery, repented, and afterward deliverance resulted.

5. Break every curse:

Through the many questions you will be asking and the transparent and honest answers and confessions, you will have a good idea of curses that need to be broken. I will usually deal with such curses with a prayer like this:

> **"In the Name of Jesus, I break this curse of (   )
> off this person. Out, in Jesus' Name!**

Parents brought their seven-year-old son to me, who still sucked his thumb like a baby. I took authority over a demon and cast it out. Any curse was broken (as was the bondage!).

6. Exorcise demons!

There is no magic formula involved. A simple, "Come out in Jesus' Name!" may be all you need. Be prepared: demons rarely come out after saying this just once. Peter bears witness to this truth:

'**Resist him, steadfast in the faith**" (1 Peter 5:9).

Even Jesus had to pray more than once to dislodge evil spirits in a man (see Luke 8:30-33). Demons know when you mean business. They will put up resistance and fight to keep from having to leave as long as their strength (or yours!) lasts.

I would like to suggest an average time it takes to set people free, but it varies so much. One thing I have learned: the sooner a person cooperates and fulfills the scriptural requirements to be free, the sooner he or she will find freedom. The longer a deliverance session takes, the more you must rely upon detection.

7. Speak to specific types of demons or grouping of demons (refer to Chapter 17).

Birds of a feather flock together. If someone has been sexually abused as a child, they likely will have a spirit of shame, rejection, guilt, or a man-hating spirit, etc. Call such things out. If a word comes to your mind, speak that. It may be just your experience, something you read (like in this book), or it just might be Holy Spirit revelation!

Your best friend in ministering deliverance is the person for whom you are praying. Explain to them,

> "If a name, a memory, a word, or an emotion comes to your spirit, stop us and tell us about it so we can work on getting that out."

They will even say things like, "He's laughing at you!" They can often "hear" what a demon is saying. If they begin to cough or gag, get a box of tissues or wastebasket. It is rare for a person to throw up much, but they may need to spit or cough up a little phlegm.

If a demon begins to manifest, you don't have to hold a person down, except to keep them from hurting themselves or others around them. Sometimes the person is in complete control during deliverance, but other times their eyes will roll back in their head, or they will jerk around. Occasionally the demon will begin speaking through them.

When demons speak through a person, they use the person's vocal box and voice, though it will be strained or somewhat eerie sounding, maybe like two voices speaking at once. It is bizarre!

8. Command demons to "manifest yourself!"

Demons try to hide and remain undetected. But if you believe what the Word says about your authority over demons, use that authority.

Demons often manifest themselves by atypical body movements or facial expressions. If there is no observable manifestation, I will continue praying for them with my hand laid upon them, commanding demons to manifest themselves. Deliverance sessions require patience!

Next, I ask the person:

"Describe what you are feeling inside. Do you feel good, bad, or nothing?"

- If they say "nothing" (after a reasonable amount of time praying), either they are already free, didn't have a demon in the first place or are not spiritually ready yet for their deliverance.

- If they say "good" they are probably delivered from at least one demon!

- If they describe sensing a very negative emotion (anger, fear, anxiety, sorrow, etc.), or if they feel a pain in their body or nausea, you know you have more warfare ahead!

Whatever they describe, pray against that, and call it out. "Anger, come out!" or "Spirit of sorrow, leave!" I will keep doing this several times, keeping up the spiritual warfare, until they say they feel nothing. Or, they often will say, "I feel peace!" Oh, that's a good sign!

Quote verses to yourself, the candidate for deliverance, and the devil, reminding all of your biblical authority to make demons leave (Matthew 12:28, Mark 16:17, Luke 10:19, James 4:7, Revelation 12:11, etc.). Fight until the candidate is. . .

EMPTY

It is amazing how many people through the years, when I asked them how they felt, they said, "empty." I don't know what on earth they mean by that unless it is the way you feel after being sick and vomiting. Regardless, it is interesting that "empty" is the exact word used by a demon, who had previously been cast out of a man, to describe the condition in which he later found him. He was "empty" (Matthew 12:44).

I assure you that many of these people who had described feeling "empty" had no idea that the word they used was the same one Jesus used. What a witness of the validity and accuracy of the scriptural ministry of deliverance.

What is the ministry of deliverance? Jesus defined it in five simple words:

"Behold, I cast out demons" (Luke 13:32).

Boldly announce the good news to the devil and the demonized. Make it your confession and proclaim it even now: "Behold, I cast out demons!"

I once read where a new convert had just discovered Mark 16:17, 18, which (as you well know by now) says believers can cast out demons. He came to his pastor and asked if it was true that even he could cast out demons. The pastor said, "Yes, you can!" The young man, now so excited, told his pastor:

"Oh, I wish I knew someone who has a demon!"

Now that you know your authority in Christ, do you wish you knew someone who has a demon? Well, YOU DO! So, the question now is:

What are you going to do about it?

MIRACLES ARE YOUR DESTINY was never intended to be an exhaustive, comprehensive study. Such would take volumes. I believe I have given you enough ammunition to wreak plenty of havoc on Satan's kingdom.

I hope you now desire to learn more about the deliverance ministry. If so, you may want to order one or more of the books listed below (all are available on Amazon.com):

Free Indeed: Deliverance Ministry, by Dr. Douglas Carr, CreateSpace Independent Publishing Platform; 2nd edition, 2013.

They Shall Expel Demons by Derek Prince, Chosen Books, Grand Rapids, 1998.

Spring the Trap by Glen and Marge Williams, Creation House Press, Lake Mary, Florida, 2004.

Blessing Or Curse (this book deals primarily with curses) by Derek Prince, Chosen Books, Grand Rapids, Michigan, 1990, 2000, 2006.

The Handbook for Spiritual Warfare Revised and Updated by Dr. Ed Murphy, Thomas Nelson, Nashville, 2003 (This is probably the most comprehensive book ever written on the subject, with nearly 600 pages, big ones, with small print!).

Do You Need Further Personal Help?

Perhaps as you read the last two chapters, you began to suspect that you need deliverance yourself. It is possible that you don't know anyone who understands and has experience in this ministry. In Chapter 20, we show how you can set yourself free through "Self-Deliverance."

If you try on your own and get "stuck" and don't know who or where to turn to for help, I highly recommend Dr. Douglas Carr. He is a personal friend and confidant, a deeply spiritual Christian, and a leading expert and author in the field of dealing with demons.

Dr. Carr pastors in Michigan, but he ministers deliverance over the phone (so you won't have to drive a great distance for help). He is a full-time minister, dependent on offerings, so charges $100.00 (Psychiatrists charge $300-$500 for an "Initial "Consultation," so that is a bargain for what you get!).

Email him to find out more at:

freedomminister@yahoo.com

19

A Haunted House

"He cried out in a loud voice: "She has fallen! Great Babylon has fallen! She is now haunted by demons and unclean spirits; all kinds of filthy and hateful birds live in her"
(Revelation 18:2 GNT).

While I was about half-way through this section on Deliverance, my wife and I received a phone call from a woman named Mary (a pseudonym) who desperately needed our help.

Their problem started with what appeared to be a malfunctioning air conditioner. The thermostat kept going up, by itself, as high as 99 degrees. Mary would wake up at night in unbearable heat. They replaced the thermostat, but the other one they installed kept doing the same thing. Then their refrigerator freezer stopped working.

Next came what they thought was a plumbing problem. Mary's nephew came over and replaced the catch at the toilet where the water seemed to be coming from. That solved nothing. Water was soon leaking from the refrigerator, the sink, and the other two bathrooms in the house, leaking from under the faucets.

After all this, water began to appear on the walls of the house. A plumber tried to figure out where the water was coming from, but it would appear from walls where there were no pipes behind them. Walls in every single room in the house began to develop water droplets on them. Next, water puddles appeared in the middle of the floors. Her nephew climbed under the raised foundation, and there were no water pipes running through the rooms. That's when they knew something was really wrong!

As if that wasn't enough, a mixture of water and oil began to form on walls. Next, Mary's 13-year-old daughter Celine (another pseudonym) found salt or sugar in the Awake and Watchtower magazines that some Jehovah Witness ladies had given her. Other piles of salt or sugar appeared.

In one pile, the word, "Hi" was written. There were words written in piles all over the house. Cinnamon and chili powder, were splattered all over the walls. Then they found toothpaste also spread on the walls and toilet bowl cleaner under the beds.

Next, their beds were soaked with water. They tried to cover them with curtains. That didn't work since, obviously, as she said, "It is not of this world." The beds would still be soaked underneath the curtains, maybe on one side, enough that they couldn't sleep where the water was.

At night, after the lights were out, Celine, as well as her grandmother, who also lived in the house, would feel water being splashed on their skin. Celine would ask her mom, "Why did you come in and splash water on me?" Of course, Mary hadn't done such a thing. It wasn't a lot of water, but enough to disturb them.

They had 5-gallon water jugs of drinking water, and several of them were tipped over. When Mary opened the kitchen cabinets, she discovered that the sugar had been spilled, the cereal was spilled, even oil was spilled. Shampoos, lotions, or nail-polish removers on the counters were open and spilled. Two new and unopened Pace Picante Sauces were opened and spilled on the pantry.

A Clorox Bleach container in the den was spilled on the floor. More oil was forming on the walls and blinds. Writing appeared scratched into the walls with words like, "My house" or "Leave." By this time, at the point of desperation, Mary phoned me.

The Declaration of War

We drove to her house to see what we could do to help her. As we sat down with Mary, Celine, and Mary's mother, we heard all that had happened in their home. It was a lovely, modern, one-story tract home in a suburb of Los Angeles (Not some 3-story, decrepit, old mansion as depicted in horror movies!). After hearing the fantastic story, I began asking some of the questions you have been reading about in earlier chapters, looking for clues as to the source of these extraordinary developments.

Mary admitted that she had a fascination with horror movies ever since she was a girl about five-years-old. She had no fear after watching such movies. (I can still remember how terrified I was in grammar school after watching such films in the 1950s, like Wolfman and Frankenstein, which were mild compared to more recent R-rated horror movies!). She had always seen what she described as "shadow people."

Neither Mary nor I could remember the exact sequence of the following events because we spent hours and several trips to both her house and her older brother's house across a timespan of several weeks. To escape this house of terror, Mary and her family moved in for a while with her brother. It was there that Celine began to see what she described as "figures just walking by her."

Demons started talking to Celine also. They would hurt the inside of her ears. She would feel them touching her back and her feet. She would sit on the floor, covering her ears, trying to get rid of what was there. The family members would tell her, "Nothing is there," but such things continued to happen.

Soon Celine said she could see "the faces" of the two Jehovah's Witnesses who had come to their house and tried to convert her. They had called her, again and again, to pressure her to let them teach her the Bible and had left those magazines. It is a lesson for Christians that their magazines became the epicenter of demonic manifestations. The faces she saw, she said, "were laughing at her. "

From there, it only got worse. Mary could "see the face of the enemy" in her own daughter's face. Celine would try to bite family members as they were praying for her. She spat on them. She ended up hurting their dog. Her strength while manifesting took Mary and Mary's sister-in-law to hold her down (And she only weighs 105-lbs!).

The demon spoke through Celine's voice and said, "I will come back, and I will be back seven times stronger." (And since her daughter was so young and had never really read the Bible, Mary knew that it wasn't Celine speaking!). Late one night, the demons seemed to be choking Celine, and she was unable to breathe. Mary was afraid the demons were killing her and panicked. So she rushed Celine to an emergency room.

While in a hospital room, after the nurses had administered drugs intravenously to calm her down, Celine came to herself and said, "Let's just go home! I know I am not crazy, and I am not sick!" So, Mary took her back home. Because in such cases, officials suspect possible child abuse, a social worker came to their home. Thankfully, the demons didn't manifest while she was there, and she saw that there was no abuse going on in the family. God was on Mary's side!

Sometimes the manifestations were like some attention-getting attempt. Celine would throw herself on the floor, but Mary would say, "You know, I've got to go to work," and turn around and walk away. At that, her daughter would get back up again. Mary said, "It was the weirdest thing. It was like it had different stages."

The first time, my wife Kathy, my son, Nathan, and I went over to pray and take authority over demons. Soon, I tried to get others involved in this warfare. I texted my intercessors to pray with us and to see if the Lord showed them anything (And they readily shared what they were picking up in their spirits). Family, friends, and fellow Christians were praying and some were fasting.

At times I alone would go over to her brother's house to help them wage warfare. We would talk about ways the enemy had gained "topos" in their house, especially in Celine's life. There were repentances, renunciations, and the bringing of traumas from the past into the open to deal with.

A Woman of God Takes Over

I am happy to report that it was my wife, Kathy, an ordained minister of the gospel, who basically "took over" the project. She met with Mary and Celine to counsel and pray with them on several occasions at their brother's home. Their learning curve was steep! I was tired and so relieved that Kathy felt led to take over much of the battle.

Through this weeks-long process, the manifestations began to be shorter and shorter. In the early stages, Mary and her family might have to pray against evil spirits for as long as four hours. More than once, they phoned us, and we came over to join them in the fight. But it was the concerned family members who spent the most time and effort in battle.

These manifestations would happen two or more times a day, then once a day until Celine finally began to join them in the fight. In one of the last manifestations, when the demon threw her on the floor, Celine would, "like a champ" (Her proud mother reports!), "pull herself up." When the demon knocked her down again, she would get back up on her knees and then her arms. This would happen several times. That's when, Mary reports, "We knew she was coming through. She was learning to overcome."

It was thrilling for Kathy and me to see Mary, her brother, and sister-in-law grow in faith and exercise their authority in Christ. After calling everyone they could think of, Mary asked me, "Maybe we need to take her to a Catholic Church for an exorcism." I told her exorcism is what we had been doing! (Probably, all those horror movies she had watched through the years made her think the Catholic Church was more into exorcism than we Protestants were. God please change this!).

Mary and her sister-in-law, on the same day, both read "Come to me" somewhere (That phrase is found several places in the gospels). They felt the Lord told them to stop looking so much to man's help and look to the Lord! They did just that because they were texting me fewer and fewer "emergency" texts about attacks. They were learning their authority in Christ. "Our faith was getting stronger," Mary reported.

One evening while they all were sitting in the kitchen, an adjacent room spontaneously caught on fire. That same day a big Teddy Bear spontaneously caught on fire. Pieces of paper in another room caught on fire twice. Celine's makeup box caught on fire. A lot of clothes caught on fire in a closet and had to be thrown out. A couch caught on fire and burned so badly they had to throw it out too.

The fires slowly wound down until they ceased entirely. There were no more manifestations in Mary's daughter. Kathy had to deal with a spirit of rebellion because previously, if Celine's mom told her to do something she didn't want to do, it triggered the demons in her. But Mary was able to discipline Celine again without serious problems. Celine is even reading the Bible now. When I asked Mary what were the lessons that she learned through all this experience and how her life had changed. She said:

> "It changed my life in that I had accepted Christ as my Lord and Savior, and I believed in God, but obviously my faith wasn't as strong as it is getting. To me, it is like the enemy is an idiot. If this nastiness exists, then obviously, God is real. It only reinforced that He is real. I have seen this. I have lived it. Every day I study and learn something new, and it is so beautiful now. I study, and I love it. It got me more

into the Word. I told my daughter, 'Don't wait 40 years to know the Lord!' Go faster; it is so beautiful, you have to know. I feel I was born again through this! I always thought I was strong, but this only made me stronger. God has always been in my life, but I never took time to get to know Him."

During this battle, I called two deliverance experts I know personally for their advice. Both said they had never seen such manifestations as this family saw in their house (Like writing on walls, water, salt, or spontaneous fires.). When they told me this, I knew that God had allowed me to get involved in this "haunted house" as a confirmation to me that I must write this book!

Why This Book is Needed

I am convinced that these kinds of amazing physical manifestations will begin to happen widespread and common in homes around the nation. It is my opinion that Revelation 12:9-12 predicts this coming time:

> **"So the great dragon was cast out, that serpent of old, called the Devil and Satan, who deceives the whole world; he was cast to the earth, and his angels were cast out with him. . . And they overcame him by the blood of the Lamb and by the word of their testimony. . . Therefore rejoice, O heavens, and you who dwell in them! Woe to the inhabitants of the earth and the sea! For the devil has come down to you, having great wrath, because he knows that he has a short time."**

The above was written thousands of years ago. Soon, these horrific goings-on will be described, in modern vernacular, as,

"All Hell is Breaking Loose!"

The thing that is so beautiful to me about this "haunting" experience was that the solution was not some super-spiritual evangelist's mighty anointing. Many of the above events were, to be honest, above my pay scale. But, thank God, they weren't above my pray scale! This was especially true when joined by the fasting and prayers of so many others. Not one man, not one woman, but the body of Christ; leaders, laymen, new converts, intercessors, and families under attack all teamed together to do battle for two households. And we won!

Mary reads the Bible every night now at 8:30 PM. Her brother began to study books on deliverance. They will never again doubt the reality of God or Satan. They have become warriors in the army of God. They will be ready to face demons in others' lives without fear. It was a great victory for the kingdom of God.

This "haunted house" was barely one mile from mine. The next haunting you hear about might be from your neighbors, right next door. After reading this section, you know what to do, don't you?

One more important observation; rarely is the problem a "haunted house." I have found that in most every case, it's the "person" who has the demon. Once they meet the conditions and are set free, the demonic manifestations in their home cease.

People have asked me to, "Come to our house and anoint it with oil." That is not a bad thing to do, of course. But deal with the person who is haunted, and the house will usually become un-haunted.

So, are you inspired? Are you excited and challenged to join God's army and wreak havoc on Satan's kingdom? A 1978 pacifist badge said. . .

"Join the Army, see the world, meet interesting people - and kill them!"

A war between nations where people kill each other may be debatable, but the ongoing conflict between God's Army and demonic powers is not. And, yes, it's a fight unto death! If not written on an actual badge, at least may it be written on your heart to invite others to. . .

"Join God's Army, see the invisible world, meet infestations of demons and defeat them!"

20

The Final Challenge

"(He) **delivered us from so great a death, and does deliver us; in whom we trust that He will still deliver us**" (2 Corinthians 1:10).

As Paul expresses above, deliverance is a past, present and future process. Some receive deliverance from one bondage, struggle with another for a period, until God then delivers them from that. You do not have to get someone completely free from every piece of baggage (Hebrews 12:1: "weights") they ever picked up, in one evening session after church (even dentists usually schedule long overdue dental work over several appointment dates).

When I am ministering deliverance and not seeing the progress I usually see, I have learned to let the candidate for deliverance go home to give the Holy Spirit some more time to reveal things that might assist them to help get free. As you read in several of the testimonies included in this book, it was while at home that the Lord revealed how and why bondages started.

Self-Deliverance

In the quiet of their home, during self-reflection, prayer, sometimes fasting, the Lord can speak a word to their heart, give them a dream, or even finish the work begun in the church. I carry in my briefcase "homework," a list of further actions they can take before I offer to meet with them again at the altar after the following service.

Following is a helpful edited list I created years ago. You have Warford Ministries' permission to photocopy and keep at hand (maybe several printed up in this book?). Give the list to a candidate for deliverance. Tell them you can share together what they have "discovered" the next time you meet again for prayer. You can also find this helpful list at my ministry website: www.deawarford.org (click on "more," then "Dea's teachings").

Discovering the Roots of Demonic Bondage

Take this list home and read over it carefully. Pray much about it, spending as much time as you can, quietly before the Lord. Fast some if you feel led to. If married, get suggestions and observations from your mate. As you pray over each section, ask the Lord to give you revelation knowledge about any of these areas where you need healing. (You may have a dream from the Lord tonight!).

Write down what comes to you in the blank space following each subject (use the back of the page if needed). Bring this completed list with you for others to help pray with you. (Bring the actual page, not just your memory!). Or, even better, if you will do all these things, you may discover freedom on your own at home! Keep in mind that there may be more than one demon (Mary Magdalene had seven! Mark 16:9). If any demons begin to manifest themselves (through coughing, jerking, nausea) plead His Blood and exert your will, refusing to let them control your body. You have authority over them (Luke 10:19).

1. FORGIVENESS: Is there anyone from your past (even going back to early childhood) or from your present that in some way hurt you and you haven't yet forgiven them? God will remind you of a name, a face, or an event. List them (If you can't remember the name, write "guy who ... etc.). Then, take time to say, "Lord, I forgive (say their name) for what they did. Forgive me for harboring anger, bitterness or unforgiveness toward them." (Matt. 6:14, 15). If it is someone who knows you have unforgiveness toward them (because of some ongoing feud), call or write them and ask for their forgiveness. (Matt. 5:23, 24). **Command any spirits of unforgiveness to leave!** (James 4:7)

2. OCCULT INVOLVEMENT: Ask the Lord to refresh your memory if there were any experiences in your past when you had anything to do with the occult, such as: witchcraft, astrology, Ouija Board, Tarot Cards, Fortune-telling ESP, mind-reading, palm reading, seances, astral projection (out-of-the-body experiences), telekinesis (moving objects with the mind), Voodoo (putting curses on people), Santeria, Satan worship, Freemasonry, Transcendental Meditation, and all false religions. List each of them and take time to renounce them one by one saying, "Lord, I renounce my involvement in (name it). Forgive me. I'll not do it again!" (II Cor. 4:20). If you have any occult books or other paraphernalia you suspect the devil might use as a means of control, throw it outside in the trash can!). **Then, command any demon power to go!**

3. SIN: Search your heart and ask the Holy Spirit to reveal any unconfessed sin or sins you have learned to live with. Write these down. In the presence of Jesus, ask Him to cover any sins with His Blood and deliver you from their power. Repent on your knees! Make a fresh commitment to overcome. **Then command any demons empowering those sins to go!**

4. <u>TRAUMATIC EVENTS</u>: (PTSD, sexual molestation, rape, horrible accidents, abandonment by a mate or a parent, loss of a loved one that you haven't been able to get over, abuse, deep hurts, childhood traumatization, etc.). As the Holy Spirit reminds you of these events, write them down. He may give you a revelatory dream. Then, on your knees, visualize Jesus stepping back with you into your past and healing you of the trauma. Ask Jesus to deliver you from all negative effects (Luke 4:18, Joel 2:32).

> **Break any curses you feel were put upon you or passed down through your family** (Galatians 3:13).

> **Command demons using these past experiences against you to go in Jesus' Name** (Mark 16:17).

5. <u>REVELATION KNOWLEDGE</u>: Ask the Lord to give you the name or type of demon that is harassing you. Ask Him the reason you may be having difficulty getting delivered. Pray much in the Spirit (in tongues) if you have your prayer language (Rom. 8:26, 27; 1 Cor. 14:2; 1 Cor. 2:10). When a name, a word, a memory or a strong emotional feeling (revealing the "type" of demon it is) comes to you, write it down. **Ask Jesus to deliver you and cast out that specific spirit!**

If you are not already completely delivered by the time you have done all of the above suggestions, your next prayer session should quickly bring deliverance! **Don't forget to bring this completed list with you.**

(That completes the list.)

While reading this you may have thought to yourself: I think I need deliverance! No problem, just do what the list says!

The Ongoing Challenge

"Now is the judgment of this world; now the ruler of this world will be cast out" (John 12:31).

In this present church age, it is our ongoing challenge to "cast out" Satan's rule and replace it with Christ's rule. We will be doing this up until the day that Christ returns and casts Satan and his demons into the bottomless pit for 1,000 years! What Christ ultimately does with demons is His business. Our business, in this age, is to cast them out!

Demons will Return!

"When an impure spirit comes out of a person, it goes through arid places seeking rest and does not find it. Then it says, 'I WILL RETURN to the house I left.'" (Matthew 12:43, 44 NIV).

Notice a demon's stubbornness: "I will return." Demons like to be in a physical body. They even preferred to live in pigs than the atmosphere (Matthew 8:31, 31).

After all the glorious victories I have shared with you in Part 2, I hate to break the bad news, but I must: Not everyone who gets set free from a demon stays free. That is why Paul wrote:

"But now that you know God. . .how is it that you want to turn back to those weak and pitiful ruling spirits? Why do you want to become their slaves all over again?" (Galatians 4:9 GNT).

I sometimes receive a report that a Christian who found glorious liberty over demonic bondage had, as Paul warned against: "become their slaves all over again." Paul added these words:

> **"I fear for you. Perhaps all my hard work**
> **with you was for nothing"** (Galatians 4:11).

Yes, sadly, sometimes our work ends up being "for nothing." Don't let that hinder you from pressing on in the fight. There are people right now weeping in hell, souls for whom Christ died, who by rejecting His offer of salvation, tragically made His work on their behalf, "for nothing."

You read earlier in Chapter 12 about the "Bible-believing, pew jumping, praise warrior, and intercessor" who got so mad that his wife said he looked like "the Incredible Hulk." He walked in freedom for a while, but later I heard the sad report that he had reverted to that same bondage, as Solomon warned:

> **"The man of great wrath will suffer**
> **punishment; for if you rescue him, you will**
> **have to do it again"** (Proverbs 19:19).

One woman from Oregon was gloriously set free from depression, and what a testimony she gave! I talked with the pastor a couple of years later, and she was then in a mental hospital!

Remember the man delivered from demons who said, "I didn't know you could be this happy as a Christian?" I told him about a man who wanted to be free from pornography and that I had dumped all his Playboy magazines into the trash can outside. After he left my office, I had a feeling, so peeked out the window towards the front of my apartment. There, I saw him digging through the trash to get the filthy magazines! Everyone makes their own choices!

A pastor told me about a woman God had delivered from self-mutilation. Afterward she walked for years in freedom. However, over a decade later, he discovered that she was back again into self-mutilation.

In one of my revival services in a Foursquare Church, a woman who manifested and screamed was set free from demons. When she told her pastor about it, he warned her, "Christians can't have demons. Come back under me and my teachings, and I'll help you." She did. Unfortunately, eventually, that demon returned. She came into bondage to fear so severely that she had to go on medication.

Many years back, a woman with a deliverance ministry prayed for me (Dea), and God delivered me from pornography. The difference afterward was amazing! I am embarrassed to admit that I opened the door again to that demon for a while. Then (thank God many years ago!), the Lord delivered me. I was finally, once and for all, free from pornography (as I shared earlier). By God's grace, I have never let that demon back inside and never will!

Mass Deliverance

After arriving at a church to conduct a revival, the pastor was helping me drag in my suitcases full of books, tapes, and T-shirts that I sold at the time (Trust me: being an evangelist is not a get-quick-rich-scheme! It is hard work!).

As he struggled with the heavy luggage, the pastor told me, "I already know I don't want to be an evangelist!" Well, that was OK with me because I already knew I didn't want to be a pastor!

The meetings were well-attended. One night, I spoke on "spiritual warfare." At the altar call, while eyes were closed, I asked people to raise their hand if they felt they probably needed deliverance. There were an unusually high percentage of people who raised their hands. I knew I wouldn't have adequate time to pray over everyone. Thus, I decided to do a "mass deliverance."

I asked everyone who knew they probably needed deliverance to come up to the front row and sit. Quite a few did. I raised my hands toward them and said:

> **"In the name of Jesus, I command any demons present in the lives of these people tonight to MANIFEST YOURSELF and come out!"**

After a short time of making such commands, all hell broke loose in that church! It was the closest thing to pandemonium I had ever seen. Not only on the front row but also seated around the audience, congregants began manifesting demons. Some were coughing; some were jerking.

A lady flopped out on the floor and screamed what seemed to be a supernaturally loud lungful of air. She repeated these screams three or four times as the demons came out! She was delivered from fear!

One woman started running away from me, heading towards the rear exit. I hollered to some men, "Don't let her leave!" Several men rose to stop her before she exited. She fell in a pile in the aisle before them.

While I was ministering to others, a newly appointed assistant minister in the church, Bill (a pseudonym), who had just recently entered the ministry, prayed over a woman whom, for privacy, we'll call "Kay." He had been counseling and praying with her in his office for some time. He tried to help her find relief. Bill knew some about the deliverance ministry but was not yet wholly equipped to do it.

Kay was being molested by her dad's homosexual "boyfriend," who was an elder at another church! He justified his abuse of her by saying that he was "trying to plant the seed of God in her."

She had been burning herself on her arms; that was how "she was driving away the pain." Kay subsequently had to go to a doctor for skin grafts. She was self-mutilating, anorexic, suicidal, and homicidal.

As Bill and others began praying for Kay, where she was seated on the front row, she began levitating out of her chair, sweat pouring off her face. They fought for her until the demons came out! The Lord marvelously filled her with the Holy Spirit that same night. After this, Kay immediately began walking with dramatic and newfound freedom.

Bill had experienced such a shocking yet exhilarating experience; he was never the same again. Now, highly motivated, he began pursuing a deliverance ministry. He didn't learn it from books; the Holy Spirit taught him.

The Lord sent Bill a prayer partner with the gift of discerning of spirits. She would even know a demon's name, when, and how it came in. She worked closely with him for a couple of years. Word got around, and people were coming from all over the country to be set free. He even trained as many as 500 people in one session on being set free from demonic bondage.

I talked with Bill on the phone recently, and he said:

> **"Every day for 15 years, 12 hours a day, I would minister deliverance to people. It was like the book of Acts!"**

To this day, he points to that service where I taught about spiritual warfare, and the power of God to deliver the oppressed was so sensationally demonstrated, as the catalyst for his deliverance ministry.

The Lord reminded me of Bill, and I looked through old records and found his cell-phone number, which hadn't changed yet, and gave him a call. I know the Lord let him retell me the above story (I had forgotten many details) so that we could use it to close out the teaching on Casting out Demons.

How to Maintain Deliverance

We shared above how even those who are wonderfully set free from demons can come back under that same old bondage. You know how important it is to teach a new convert how to walk with the Lord and not fall back into his old sinful ways. Similarly, it's essential to help those who are delivered to maintain deliverance.

> **"When an unclean spirit goes out of a man, he goes through dry places, seeking rest, and finds none. Then he says, 'I will return to my house from which I came.' And when he comes, he finds it empty, swept, and put in order. Then he goes and takes with him seven other spirits**

more wicked than himself, and they enter and dwell there; and the last state of that man is worse than the first" (Matthew 12:43-45).

Notice the word "empty." No demons were there, and it adds that the person's insides were "swept, and put in order." The KJV says, "garnished." In other words, it was ready for a tenant to take over the "topos." The man had not continued to move towards wholeness and holiness and, instead, had hung a sign out that said, "House to let: demons welcome."

Note also that it says the demon brought seven other demons with him who "were more wicked than himself."

This phrase "more wicked" proves that some demons are worse than others (perhaps this is why some depressed people sit around being miserable while others go out and kill people!).

Some have suggested that an "empty" place needs to be filled with the Holy Spirit. And so, they will pray with the delivered person to receive the Holy Spirit. It is then thought that once filled with the Spirit, that demon will find it harder to come back in again.

However, as you read in the testimonies in this book, many who found freedom were already filled with the Holy Spirit! So, I know by experience that being filled with the Holy Spirit, though vastly important, is not a guarantee that no demon can ever come back. Remember, deliverance is for Christians (even Spirit-filled Christians!).

Once free, how can one maintain their deliverance? It isn't rocket science. . .

1. Stay in the Word of God:

Attend church services and Bible studies. Read the Word, memorize it, confess it, pray it, and speak it to the enemy when he sneaks back! Three times the devil spoke to Jesus in Matthew 4 and Luke 4, and each time the Lord answered him by quoting a verse of Scripture saying:

"It is written."

As I said, it isn't rocket science!

> **"By the word of Your lips, I have kept away from the paths of the destroyer"** (Psalm 17:4).

The last day battle will especially require a steadfast dependence on the Word:

> **"And they overcame him by the blood of the Lamb and by the WORD OF THEIR TESTIMONY"** (Revelation 12:11).

Let your "testimony" always be, "No Satan. I am delivered by the blood of the Lamb. I will not come back under your bondage. Go, in the Name of Jesus!"

2. Stay in Prayer:

There is a good reason why, when Jesus taught the disciples The Lord's Prayer, He told them to pray:

> **"deliver us from the evil one"** (Matthew 6:13).

Prayer is a primary tool to stay delivered from both sin and the devil!

> **"Watch and pray, lest you enter into temptation"** (Matthew 26:41).

3. Stay in fellowship with other believers:

In Chapter 19, you saw how a mother unwittingly let her daughter study with Jehovah's Witnesses, and you read what happened as a result!

It is in the context of being among church family members that James 5:16 says:

> **"Confess your trespasses to one another, and pray for one another."**

We were warned in Hebrews 10:24, 25:

> **"And let us consider one another in order to stir up love and good works, not forsaking the assembling of ourselves together...but exhorting one another."**

Assemble "together" often! We need each other, and that will especially be true in the coming last days, the time of "the final challenge" of the church versus the devil.

Finally, respect Paul's "fear" in 2 Corinthians 11:3:

> **"But I fear, lest somehow, as the serpent deceived Eve by his craftiness, so your minds may be corrupted from the simplicity** ("full and pure devotion to Christ" GNT) **that is in Christ."**

Simplicity. That means again that it isn't rocket science. Love God, love the Bible, love prayer, love the body of Christ, and MAINTAIN GOOD WORKS:

> **"This is a faithful saying, and these things I**

want you to affirm constantly, that those who have believed in God should be careful to maintain good works" (Titus 3:8).

The dramatic story of Bill and Kay and her night of deliverance vividly illustrates the primary purpose of Part 2 of this book: you can and will cast out demons!

> **"The Lord RAISED UP a deliverer for the children of Israel, who delivered them"**
> (Judges 3:9).

The Lord "raised up a deliverer" named Dea.

Then he "raised up a deliverer" named Bill.

Is it now time for you to be "raised up" to be a "deliverer?"

Deliverance will be a ministry in high demand in the coming last days. Thus, in closing the largest chunk of this book, dedicated to casting out demons, may I ask: Will you be ready for. . .

The Final Challenge!

PART Three

PROPHESYING

"Dear Dea,

Thank you for ministering here at Coastlands Community Church again this year. We have been applying many of the things you taught us last year and have been experiencing a wonderful flow of the Holy Spirit. As I reflected on the past 13 months since you ministered on using the prophetic anointing of the Spirit to advance the Kingdom, I realized that I have prophesied more in that period than in all of my life combined. It has become an area of strength rather than an area of weakness. You continued to encourage us with the prophetic words you received from the Lord and ministered to individual people during your ministry here. The words were very accurate and meaningful for our church family members. Thank you for being obedient."

From Pastor Durant Kreider,
Coastlands Community Church, Chesapeake, Virginia

21

How to Prophesy

"You can all prophesy"
(1 Corinthians 14:31).

Prophesy is the verb form of the noun prophecy. Prophecy is the ability to speak words inspired by God. Those spoken words can address a person, giving them counsel or enlightenment for a present or past circumstance (often referred to as "forthtelling"). Prophetic words also can be "foretelling" the future. The manifestation of this amazing ability is called "prophesying." And guess what?

You can Prophesy! I didn't say it, God did! In 1 Cor. 14:31, Paul wrote in a letter to the Corinthian church members the following words:

"You can all prophesy."

You (in the original Greek language) means YOU!

Can means CAN.

All means ALL.

And prophesy means PROPHESY!

Now (my nitpicky friends), I admit that in this context, it probably is referring to those with the office of a prophet (see verses before and after). However there are ample other scriptures to indicate that God can use anyone to prophesy. Proof of this is the fact that in the same letter to the entire Corinthian church, Paul wrote things like:

> **"Desire spiritual gifts; but especially that you may prophesy"** (14:1).

> **"Desire earnestly to prophesy"** (14:39).

Also, the **"gift of prophecy"** is listed along with other gifts of the Spirit (12:7-11) as available, **"for the profit of all"** (12:7).

Some people think that prophesying is something that only prophets do. Prophets do specialize in this gift (as their "title" intimates), even as evangelists specialize in taking the good news to unsaved people. Yet, just as every Christian can "do the work of an evangelist" (2 Tim. 4:5) and witness to others concerning the gospel, so too, every Christian can be used of God to prophesy to others.

That this is an essential gift which we all should diligently seek to be operational in our life is proven by the fact that Paul urged the church in 14:1 to:

> **"Desire spiritual gifts** (then quickly added),

> **"but ESPECIALLY that you may prophesy."**

Prophecy is an ESPECIALLY important gift and always has been since the early history of God's dealings with humanity. Enoch was the first person in history that we know prophesied (Jude 14). Abraham, the "Father of faith," was the first known prophet (Gen. 20:7). Moses was a prophet (Deut. 34:10). In fact, most every book of the Old Testament was written by a prophet. We truly owe the very existence of our faith, to a great extent, to the ministry of the Prophet!

Even as the Old Testament could not have been written without the contributions of the prophets, so also, the New Testament Church owes its very roots to the prophets:

> **"You, too, are built upon the foundation laid by the apostles and prophets"** (Ephesians 2:20 GNT).

Legalistic dispensationalists (a school of theologians) argue that miracles, apostles, and prophets were limited to the New Testament Church period and are no longer needed or even in existence today. This theory doesn't make sense in light of Scriptures like 1 Corinthians 12:28:

> **"And God has appointed these in the church: first apostles, second prophets, third teachers, after that miracles, then gifts of healings, helps, administrations, varieties of tongues."**

If Prophets and miracles have been done away with, why do we still have teachers, helpers, and administrators in churches today? And why do over 600 million people on earth today speak in tongues? The answer is simple: the dispensationalists are wrong! People started prophesying from at least the 7th generation from Adam, prophesied throughout the Old Testament, into the book of Acts, and are still prophesying today. I know because,

I prophesy!

I was 17 years of age and a freshman at LIFE Bible College in Los Angeles. I had a job working for FGBMFI (Full Gospel Businessmen's Fellowship) in downtown LA. Sometimes we would have a little chapel service together. We had a guest speaker (I'll call "G.") one day at work who taught about the gift of prophecy. He probably (it was a long time ago) quoted 1 Cor. 14:13:

"Therefore let him who speaks in a tongue pray that he may interpret."

G. taught that any Christian could speak in tongues and afterward interpret "by faith" what they had said. Then, he asked if anyone would like to try to do just that. One woman raised her hand, so he had her come up front and sit in a chair ("the hot seat," a common practice back during the "Charismatic Movement").

G. instructed her to pray in tongues for a moment. After she did, he stopped her and said, "Now interpret it!" I can still hear her as though it were yesterday (kind of comical!). She said, "Yea . . . Yea . . . YEA . . . " but just couldn't get any further with the interpretation. Nobody else dared to come forward after this embarrassing display, and that was the meeting.

While working, I ran (God-incidentally) into G. in the hall and confided, "When you were having that woman do that, I felt like I could have spoken in tongues and interpreted it." You didn't say something like that to a Charismaniac! He answered. "Why, do it now!" So, obligingly, right in the hall near where other people worked, I spoke with tongues momentarily. Then, I "interpreted" it.

I don't remember what all I said, but it was something about the fact that God's gifts were "for his children's usage still today." I had passed through a faith barrier and for likely the first time in my life, exercised a gift of the Spirit. Within weeks, I was giving an interpretation of a tongue at my home church.

After I gave the interpretation, I asked my girlfriend, at the time, Mary, what she thought of my interpretation. She said, "It sounded to me like you were making it up." (Thank God, He had another girl in mind to help encourage me in the work to which He had called me!) Periodically God continued to use me in giving messages in tongues and/or interpretations.

Everything you always wanted to know about prophecy but were afraid to ask

It was a long process for me to understand the operation of the gift of prophecy. I would learn that "Tongues plus interpretation of tongues equals prophecy." Paul reveals this truth in 1 Cor. 14:5:

> **"I wish you all spoke with tongues, but
> even more that you prophesied; for he who
> prophesies *is* greater than he who speaks
> with tongues, UNLESS indeed he interprets,
> that the church may receive edification."**

Prophesying is greater than speaking in tongues "UNLESS" it is interpreted. The obvious corollary of this truth is that tongues plus interpretation of tongues is the equivalent of prophecy. So, I determined, if a prophecy is the same as tongues and interpretation, why speak in tongues first? Why not move immediately into prophecy? The Lord subsequently has occasionally used me to prophesy as I sensed His Spirit inspiring me.

Since prophecy is one of the gifts of the Holy Spirit (1 Cor. 12:7-11), and we are promised in Luke 11:13 . . .

> **"the Father will "give the Holy Spirit to them that ask."**

. . . we know that we have a right to ask for and expect this gift! Concerning the Holy Spirit, we are promised:

> **"Seek and you will find"** (Luke 11:9).

If we haven't "found" prophecy, it is probably because we haven't been "seeking" it. Today begin seeking God that He might use you to prophesy!

But, you might ask: "How will I know when God is using me to prophesy? Does God move my mouth and form words while I just stand mesmerized? Does He show me something like a ticker-tape that I just read? Does He speak exact words in my ear that I simply repeat? Or is it not so simple?" It is not so simple!

Dr. Bill Hammon (kind of the granddaddy of the personal prophecy movement in America) says that we either **see, hear, or feel** prophecy. Let's examine those three "methods" the Holy Spirit uses to manifest prophecy. . .

See

In the Old Testament, prophets were called "Seers." They saw visions or had dreams. The Lord may give you a prophetic word by showing you a vision or a dream. However, this is the exception. Usually, when a prophecy comes to you as something you "see," what you see is with your spirit through your imagination (or "mind's eye"), and it comes without your routine thinking processes.

It often comes unexpectedly and intuitively. In other words, you won't imagine things about a person in a typical way. You will "see' with your spirit and not your brain (except, of course, as the Spirit always has to use your brain to process images!). This is not easy to learn and took me time.

Once a couple stood before me. The woman was pregnant. As I prayed for her, I "saw" a picture in my mind of a pink rattle (not the kind of thing that would usually come to your mind). I told them what I saw. And yes, she had a girl (I'm at least 50% accurate in my prophecies!)

I sometimes see "mental pictures" in my mind and then step out in faith to describe what I feel the picture means. (This is probably the spiritual equivalent of what psychologists call the "visual learner." They learn by "seeing things.")

If you "see" something in an unusual way, pray about it. Perhaps approach a person explaining, "I believe I see something in my spirit. May I share it with you, and you can pray about it?" If it came from your own mind, it will soon be forgotten by both you and the person you share it with. But, if it's from the Lord, it could be a word that will encourage; if not now, later.

Hear

(This could be the spiritual equivalent of the "audio-learner," the person who learns best by hearing) If the Lord gives you a prophetic word this way, you might hear the audible voice of God, like Samuel (1 Sam. 3) who thought God's voice was Eli speaking to him.

Samuel kept going into Eli's room to see what he wanted until Eli, at last, discerned that the Lord was speaking to the boy prophet.

The Lord spoke audibly to people many times in the Bible and still does today. Yet, I have served God all my adult life and never heard His audible voice. However, I have heard His voice speaking to my heart, as you have.

I "hear" words. For instance, I was in a service in Iowa. As I was looking, momentarily, at a woman in the audience (my eyes scan from one person to another while I preach). The two words "a man" came to me. I shared those words with her and told her that I didn't know if it meant a romantic relationship, a doctor, or an employer, but that I believed the Lord was going to bring "a man" into her life.

She emailed me that same week and said that a woman visiting the same service had a "word" before I gave that word: that the Lord was bringing a man romantically into her life. Again, this word was just a "whisper" to my spirit. And that isn't the best way to explain it. Only those who have had the experience understand what I mean. You too can have the same experience!

When you "hear" a word for someone, humbly share it with them: "You know, I believe the Lord may have spoken something to my heart about you."

Tell them what you "heard" and encourage them to pray and see if they get a witness to it.

Feel

(This could be the spiritual equivalent of the "hands-on-learner.") When the gift of prophecy operates in this way, you will "feel" something inside your spirit. It doesn't come in words, necessarily, but you "sense" something. You might experience a distinct emotion. It could be love, peace, fear, great joy, or a foreboding.

If you are talking or looking at someone and you "feel" something; share it with them. Try to interpret what you feel the Lord is wanting to reveal to them through the lens of what you are feeling (He loves them, they need to stop worrying, the Lord is giving them joy, etc.)

Only those who "feel" things clearly understand what I am saying. If this is how the Lord uses you, pray for God to use this "intuitive" strength you have been given by Him for the benefit of others.

I Feel Things, at Times

In a church in New Mexico, I "felt" that some woman in the church couldn't have children, and while I was quickly processing this in my mind, I noticed a woman in the church and "felt" that she was the one. I asked, "Are there any women here who can't have children but want them? Come up here now, and I will pray for you." Nobody responded.

I next said, "Maybe it is your husband that can't have children. But, come up if you want prayer." Nobody responded. A little later, I called that same woman up so we could minister to her.

As she was coming up, I asked her if the girl in front of her was her daughter. She said yes, but then said, "But my husband can't have children." Flabbergasted that she hadn't responded to what the Lord had shown me, I called her husband up and prayed for them that they might have children.

The pastor told me afterward that when he heard me give that word, he too felt that the same woman was the woman that should have responded to the word in the first place. This was a second witness.

I didn't see or hear anything. I just "felt", "sensed" that there was someone there who couldn't have children.

I had a similar experience when I was ministering at the Crescent City, California, Foursquare Church. A man, Donnie Mattz, a friend from years before, and his wife (whom I had never met), came up to the platform for prayer. As they were approaching me, I "knew" they wanted to have a child. That was precisely why they came for prayer.

I laid hands on them and prayed over their request. As they were stepping off the platform, I said, "And if it is a boy, name him, Dea." Well, guess what? They had a boy! Unfortunately, to my chagrin, the mother's name was "Dee" (what were the odds!). Still, they did give their son the middle name, "Dea."

If you "feel" or "sense" something in your spirit about someone, humbly share it with them and trust it will be eventually revealed if you're hearing from God correctly.

Prophesying Requires Faith

Whether you see, hear, or feel something, it will seldom come so powerfully that there is not a shadow of a doubt that you are getting a prophetic revelation from God. If this were true, then Paul would not have had to warn those with the gift of prophecy to:

> **"Having then gifts differing according to the grace that is given to us, let us use them: if prophecy, let us prophesy in proportion to our faith"** (Romans 12:6).

I recommend when you start prophesying, always preface your words with: "I believe the Lord is showing me. . ." This way, you, upfront, are humbly letting the person know that you could be mistaken. You are also fulfilling the above verse by prophesying "In proportion to" your faith.

If prophecies were unconditionally accurate, there wouldn't be any faith involved. The Scripture. . .

> **"We walk by faith and not by sight"**
> (II Cor. 5:7). . .

. . .is just as true about prophecy (or any other gift of the Spirit) than it is about every other aspect of the "faith" to which we are called. Prophesying is a walk of faith!

If you let pride or fear keep you from taking a chance of being wrong, you will "quench the Spirit" (1 Thess. 5:19) and stop the flow of the Holy Spirit's gift moving through you. If you wait until you are 100% sure that you are right in your prophetic word, you will likely never prophesy. Sometimes people tack on a "Thus saith the Lord!" to their word. That doesn't add a bit of authority or accuracy to the prophecy. Either you did or didn't hear correctly. Time will tell!

> **"We know in part and prophecy in part"**
> (1 Cor. 13:9).

Sometimes we only get a "part" of what the Lord is saying to our spirit.

> **"We have this treasure in earthen vessels that the excellency of the power may be of God and not of us."** (II Cor. 4:7).

Messages from God must be translated through "earthen vessels." We are fallen creatures and sometimes our flesh (our fallen intellect, emotions and will) can get in the way of what God longs to communicate through us.

As Fallen Beings. . .

Our Intellect can get in the way because we are not able to verbalize very well what we are feeling. That is why God doesn't call people with Down syndrome to be preachers of the gospel. Their intellect will prevent them from adequately verbalizing what God puts in their spirit. (They can be gloriously saved. They just can't be glorious preachers, teachers, or prophets.)

Our intellect can also get in the way because we use our normal thought processes to reason our way out of giving a word ("They won't receive it. They don't like me. I already know them, so they'll think I'm prophesying out of my own knowledge, etc.") Or, just as bad, our imaginations may get "carried away," thinking up things without God's input!

Our Emotions can hinder our prophecies because fear can grip our hearts, preventing us from stepping out in faith. Anger may cause us to prophesy with a tendency to speak harsh, judgmental words. Sympathy may push us toward adding "comforting words" to "soften" what we see and to say "nicer" things to make one feel better.

Our Will can hinder the accuracy of our prophetic words because one may be by nature very bold and rather unsympathetic. Thus, he or she may say things "by faith" which are, in reality, born out of pride or self-confidence. Also, in stubbornness, one may simply refuse to obey God and prophesy what God wants them to say.

Thus, because of our human limitations, we must always expect our prophetic words to be a "part" of the picture. Often, words are part God and part us.

Close like a Hand Grenade

I once had a preacher call me out of the audience of a big church I was visiting and ask me if my name was "Dees." It wasn't, of course, but it was close enough that I knew he had heard from God. I felt very loved of the Father that He knew my name and would call me out of this big crowd. (Though when filtered through the guest speaker's brain it became "Dees" instead of Dea).

Another time a prophet called me out from a good-sized crowd and told me and the congregation that I was very interested in "linguistics." At that time, as a non-Spanish speaker, I was desperately studying Spanish in a community college to learn the language as quickly as I could. I had recently been appointed pastor of a Spanish Church (along with pastoring the English congregation sharing the building). I knew He was a true prophet after he said that!

Then, he added, "And the Lord is healing your knee." There wasn't a single thing wrong with my knee! But, I said nothing and walked away with further evidence that we all "prophecy in part." Just accept the fact that you may be right about one word and wrong about another. If we know this, it will keep us humble and always trying to discern the mind of Christ more accurately (1 Cor. 2:16).

Don't Throw Out the Baby!

Many churches have proverbially "thrown out the baby with the bathwater!" They have all but stopped having prophecies or even tongues and interpretation of tongues during services because it is so bluntly evident that we "prophesy in part." But, by so doing, I am afraid that the enemy has deprived Christ's body of a much-needed gift! I learned long ago to appreciate the "in part" prophecies.

If I hear a prophecy in a service, I'll try to find at least one remark that resonates with my spirit. I will "receive" the truth and inspiration in that one phrase and act upon it. If the phrase, for instance, is "Praise Me," I might start praising Him right then. If it's "repent," I'll think of something about which I need to repent!

When I was a pastor and someone prophesied in my church, I might afterward give a little instruction about the prophecy and "interpret" what I felt the Holy Spirit might be communicating to the church through that word. Prophecy is God endeavoring to say something through imperfect earthen vessels. A teaching gift helps us understand what God's is saying.

Some people hear poor grammar or maybe a nugget of "erroneous theology" in some words and then categorically reject the whole word. Because of the difficulty in dealing with prophecies that are "in part," many churches have moved more and more away from encouraging the open exercise of the vocal gifts of the Spirit. I believe this happened for the following reasons:

1. It is embarrassing when you have visitors who aren't used to vocal gifts of the Spirit being openly shared.

2. Some do not exercise self-control or use wisdom in how they manifest the gift (i.e. interrupt the flow of a service or get overly emotional, or too loud).

3. Through the years, some prophecies or tongues and interpretation of tongues degenerated into so many cliché phrases, such as, "Praise me my people for I dwell in the midst of My church. I am coming soon, etc." (Even a wonderful truth like "Jesus loves you" can become cliché if overused and lose its impact in witnessing!)

Despite any seemingly viable excuses to discourage "in part" prophecies, we nevertheless must never forget Paul's words:

> **"Despise not prophesyings; prove all things;**
> **hold fast that which is good"** (1 Thess. 5:19 KJV).

We must never let our "sophistication," our "intellectualism," our desire for visitors to want to come back to our church, or our insistence on "doctrinal purity" cause us to "despise" the human weaknesses so evident in the display of the prophetic gift. "Prove all things" reminds us that we have the right, and obligation, to test any spiritual gift, as long as we remember to "hold fast that which is good." Some "good" thing can be found in almost any prophecy!

And, if it can't, in grace, allow those who are attempting to prophesy to make mistakes and grow in their gift. Some prophetic ministries give people scriptures, believing that these are special promises applicable specifically to that person. If we prophesy scripture, we'll never, ever miss it!

> **"Let two or three prophets speak and let the others judge."** (1 Cor. 14:29):

Prophecies can and should be "judged." Yet, this doesn't mean to categorically judge, "That prophecy was from Satan! You're just speaking out of your own flesh. etc." Instead, it means that we have the same Spirit in us that speaks through people (1 Jn. 2:27). Our spirit can judge those parts of a "word" that are right on and those which are maybe just off a little.

False or Inaccurate?

You might ask, "But, what about Matt. 7:15 which warns against false prophets?" Valid question!

> **"Beware of false prophets who come to you in sheep's clothing, but inwardly they are ravenous wolves":**

Here, Jesus refers to evil, deceptive, satanically led men and women. Spirit-filled, mature, sincere, and submitted brothers and sisters in Jesus are NOT "inwardly ravenous wolves." They are not going to give "false" (motivated by evil intent) prophecies. However, they may give "inaccurate" prophecies. Distinguish (with the "mind of Christ") between deceptive FALSE prophecies and those that are guilelessly INACCURATE.

If someone allows the devil to speak through them, the pastor or elders in the body can quickly put a stop to it (though I never had to do this in fifteen years of pastoring. Satan knows churches where he will be exposed!). Hebrews 13:17 give us good guidance:

"Obey them that have the rule over you in the Lord and submit yourselves, for they give an answer for your souls (Heb. 13:17).

If you long to be used in this gift of prophecy, a good starting place is to let your pastor know about your desire. Get his permission to exercise it during services. Any wise and secure pastor would be tickled to help you grow in your gift. On the other hand, if your pastor doesn't want you to use the gift, maybe you need to prayerfully determine if you are attending the right church!

If someone gives you a prophecy, what should you do with it?

First: Neither entirely accept nor reject it. Write it down. Record it with your cell phone if you can. Pray about it. See if the Lord witnesses it to your heart. Did they hit it in some areas but miss it in others? In the places where they "hit it," act on them or "pray through" concerning them.

"Son Timothy, remember the prophecies which went before on you, that by them you might wage a good warfare. Holding faith" (1 Tim. 1:18, 19).

Reread your prophecy from time to time. If it is a future promise, pray for its fulfillment. If it is a "wait and see" prophecy, then patiently wait and see. When I told that woman that "a man" was coming into her life, I hope she prayed about the word: "Lord, are you wanting to bring a man into my life?" And if she wanted a husband, I hope she more diligently and with more faith began praying to the Lord to bring that right man to her.

If she "happened" to meet "a man" in the next few months, that word would bring encouragement to her that God was guiding her and looking out for her. If she doesn't meet "a man" for twenty years, well, she'll know I missed it (And I'll avoid going back to that church!).

Notice also that Paul told Timothy to "Remember the prophecies." The inference is that sometimes words take time to be fulfilled, thus we must be patient and vigilant about prophetic words and mindful of what the Lord has said. Perusing prophecies we have received helps keep us encouraged and in prayer about it.

Second: Ask the Lord for a witness.

> **"In the mouth of two or three witnesses shall every Word be established"** (II Cor. 13:1).

Did God lead you to some verse in your devotional reading that bears witness? Does the Holy Spirit bear witness to your heart? Do you receive other words or counsel that say similar things? Prophecies need confirmation.

Third: When you are convinced that a prophecy is a word from the Lord, move in faith in expectation of its fulfillment.

The phrase in 1 Timothy 1:19 "holding faith" shows that it may take a long period of standing in faith until a word is fulfilled. Hold on to your promise! Plan for it. Save for it, etc.

Paul told Timothy in Verse 18 that the prophecies Timothy had received would help him "wage the good warfare." Prophecies aren't automatically fulfilled. Often there is a "war" involved. Your war, soldier of the Cross, might require obedience, faith, action, or actively resisting Satan's attempts to stop your forward progress. Prophecies often reveal your destiny. Satan despises your destiny!

Finally, prophecies given through the prophetic gift are not sure promises, as are Bible Promises.

Prophecies are a potential.

Prophecies are a possibility.

Prophecies are invitations to advance further in the Kingdom of God and His plan for us all. One sure thing you can depend on after this study:

The Word of God Invites YOU to Prophesy!

22

The Purpose of Prophesying

"But the one who prophesies speaks to people for their strengthening, encouraging and comfort" (1 Corinthians 14:3 NLT)

My son, Nathan, worked for Harvest International Ministries, Pastor Chae Ahn, Harvest Rock Church, Pasadena, California. One aspect of his job was to welcome visiting speakers, show them around the facilities, and acquaint them with protocols. During a special conference, Nathan welcomed a guest speaker, Shawn Bolz, and showed him around.

After the service was in progress, while Nathan was performing his duties in the foyer, over the loud-speaker system, he heard Shawn say, "Where is Nathan?" With that, Nathan ran down the aisle as soon as he could and leaped up to the platform. Shawn is a prophet and receives remarkable words, like people's names, from the Lord.

Shawn asked Nathan, "Who is Wayne?" My son said, "That is my middle name and my father's middle name."

Then Shawn said, (to the whole congregation, thinking a word was likely for someone else), "Who is Kathryn Louise?" While still standing beside Shawn, Nathan told him, "That is my mother's name." At that, Shawn told him to tell his mother, "She has great hope!"

Kathy had been going through a very difficult trial, wrestling against hopelessness. There were probably a thousand people in that conference, and my wife wasn't even at the service, but the Lord knew where she was and knew details about her life, even her middle name! When my son returned home and told her the word, you can imagine what encouragement and comfort it brought to her. She held on to the word, and today she is a woman of hope!

The Primary Goals of Prophecy

The primary goals of prophecy are to do three things:

1. Strengthen (other translations say "edification," which means "to build up")

2. Encourage (other translations say "exhortation")

3. Comfort (This means don't "expose" their SINS! Some erroneously think this is a major purpose of prophecy. There are, however, exceptions to this rule! Read below. . .)

God loves His children and wants them to be blessed by the usage of the gifts of the Spirit towards our brothers and sisters in Christ (strengthening, encouraging, and comforting). Yet, because the heart of God is always towards the lost, it is possible to walk with God in such a strong prophetic anointing, that your prophecy can be a "sign" reaching beyond your Christian family members to sinners or the unchurched.

Jesus knew by the Spirit and told an unsaved woman that she had been married five times and lived with a man who wasn't her husband (See John 4). It made such a believer out of the Samaritan woman that she spread the news of Jesus throughout her town:

> **"Many of the Samaritans from that town believed in him because of the woman's testimony, 'He told me everything I ever did.'"**

A town experienced a mighty revival because of one prophetic word. It's called "Power Evangelism." A most effective method of evangelism is to use the gifts of the Spirit, such as prophecy or healing, as a "sign" to unbelievers. Sometimes when we give a prophetic word, we might technically be manifesting one of the closely related gifts of "word of wisdom, word of knowledge, or discerning of spirits." Which exact gift is in demonstration is not important, but what is important are the results these gifts can bring.

Paul shows us the highest order of the gift of prophecy in a church service in 1 Cor. 14:24, 25:

> **"If all prophesy, and an unbeliever or an uninformed person comes in, he is convinced by all, he is convicted by all. And thus the secrets of his heart are revealed; and so, falling down on *his* face, he will worship God and report that God is truly among you."**

Sinners and visitors to a church service ("unbelievers or an uninformed person") need to repent. They need to fall under the conviction of the Holy Spirit. We all have seen this happen after the preaching of the Word of God and an altar call. But there is, as shown above, another approach: prophetic words!

"thus the secrets of his heart are revealed."

The Lord has shown me "secrets" about people. Let me share these as examples of how the Lord can use the prophetic gift to turn hearts towards the Lord.

To Be, or Not to Be. . .

God gave me a word for a man in a service in Minnesota. As I looked at him before I had even come to the pulpit, I heard in my spirit "Shakespeare." Then the line from Shakespeare's *Hamlet* came to me: "To be, or not to be, that is the question."

As he sat with his wife, I shared from the pulpit this prophecy to him: "To be or not to be, that is the question. You are in the throes of making an important decision, and you need to make sure that you are getting the Lord's direction in that decision." I noticed that they seemed unhappy and didn't crack a smile while I preached. When I gave the altar call, he raised his hand to get right with God.

Later at the altar, with his wife at his side, he told me that he and his wife were planning to counsel with the pastor after the service because he was "trying to decide if I should stay with my wife or leave her for this other woman." God, knowing this, warned him through a prophetic word, the fulfillment of: "the secrets of his heart are revealed."

A Strange Word: Calypso

In Ohio, the Lord gave me a strange word for a man I noticed seated with the congregation. The term was "Calypso." I didn't know what a Calypso was, but I thought it was a Latin musical instrument or a dance. I looked up the definition on my iPhone dictionary: "Calypso = Classical Mythology. A sea nymph who kept Odysseus on the island of Ogygia for seven years."

During my sermon, I stopped long enough to share that word with him and the rest of the congregation. I then asked him, "Have you ever spent time in prison?" He said, "Yes." I asked, "How long?" He answered, "Seven years." I had the pastor read the definition still showing on my iPhone as proof that the Lord had spoken to me precisely what I was describing.

I then prophesied about God's care for him through that time in jail and his need to serve God. When I gave the altar call, he came forward to get right with God! If you could have seen him kneeling humbly at the altar, it would have caused you to rejoice, as it did me. And it would motivate you to seek the gift of prophecy more diligently!

The following service, the man came back again. I asked him before the church, "When I gave you that word, what did you feel?" He said, "Fear!"

> **"The fear of the Lord is the beginning of wisdom"** (Proverbs 9:10).

Prophecy can be a vehicle for a "word of wisdom" to help produce "the fear of the Lord" in the unsaved, backslidden, and uncommitted.

A Word of Warning

Throughout the Old Testament, prophets warned God's people of impending doom if they didn't repent. God still does this today. When I was a youth minister, a young man named Grant, whom I had led to the Lord, lived with my parents and me. One evening he was acting wickedly and angrily. I forget what he was planning to do that night, but I gave him a word of warning, something to the effect: "A bad thing is going to happen tonight. The Lord is going to chasten you!" He scoffed and drove away determined.

It wasn't long into his night of backsliding when one of Grant's wheels fell off his car, bringing his night of rebellion to a screeching halt! Don't you think he had a little more fear of the Lord after that experience! Fulfilled prophecies can become a solid influence to encourage struggling saints or rebuke the rebellious.

A Lie Revealed

While pastoring in Walla Walla, Washington, I went door to door witnessing. At one house, I led a young woman to Christ who then began attending our church. One Sunday morning, as the church members were kneeling in prayer, I walked back to her row and laid hands on her to pray. The prophetic words came out of my mouth:

> **"Three days ago, somebody lied to you. And the Lord warns you to not listen to them."**

She afterward admitted that she had gone to a dance (probably in a sleazy bar). When the service was over, she kept saying, "How did he know that?! How did he know that?!" Of course, I knew it prophetically. That word helped produce the fear of God in her soul!

A Boy Named Alex

As you read these stories, you are probably reading more examples of the manifestation of the gift of the "word of knowledge" than prophecy. The two gifts are so closely intertwined that I hardly think we need to know which gift is operating through us. Just do it, whichever it is!

I was preaching in a small town in the Midwest. I dislike staying in old-fashioned, small, ma and pa, motels (I could tell you some stories!). There were few to choose from, so I ended up staying in one. Motel managers no longer hand out keys for their guests to lose, but this one still did.

After an evening service, I stood at my motel room in the interior corridor and reached into my pocket to find my key. It was gone! I retraced my steps, looked in my car and the area around it, but my key was nowhere to be seen. I looked across the street toward the manager's home but didn't want to announce to them at this late hour that the idiot preacher from California had lost his key!

I fumbled a few minutes at the door, debating what to do, when two women from down the hall came towards me. The brazenly way one of the women approached me, to be honest, I thought she was maybe a prostitute. I quickly explained why I was loitering at my door, telling them that I was an evangelist speaking in a church in town.

The prostitute-like woman said, "Oh, pray for me. I need prayer!" I, of course, was happy to do that and laid my hands on her to pray. Soon, the words came to my spirit and I said: "I rebuke Alex!" At first, I thought Alex was the name of a demon, but then, astonished, she said, "How did you know that? My son's name is Alex!" She then described how she and her son were estranged, and she hadn't seen him in years. I then told her that if she will turn to the Lord and serve him that the Lord will restore her relationship with Alex. I never saw her again, but she had been confronted by the Spirit of God and knew it!

A Very Difficult Word

Sometimes our obedience to the Lord is tested. My sister, Elaine, her husband, and I had come to Kentucky to minister in services. My sister walks in the office of a prophet. Pastors have reported: "Elaine read the mail of my people." She could walk down a line of people and probably give a "word" to every one of them. I learned much about prophecy from her. I am sharing some of that knowledge with you.

The three of us were standing with the pastor and his wife after the Sunday AM service in the line at Captain D's restaurant. There was a long line of people that day. I was standing directly in front of an older couple. The woman was dressed nicely, and I inquired if they had been to a church service. She had but he had not. We passed some time away by exchanging light conversation.

I had to use the restroom so I stepped away from the line for a few minutes. In the restroom, I felt concern for the man to whom I had been talking. I discerned that he was likely unsaved (typical of so many men: dropping the wife off at church, going home to watch television, then picking her up after the service to go out and eat). I asked the Lord, "Lord, do you have a word for that man?" Immediately, I "heard" a word in my spirit. It was:

HORNY!!!!!

I hadn't heard that erotic word in quite a while! How could I walk up to a virtual stranger and give THAT word? I got back in line again, and after getting my food, I sat down with my family and the pastors and shared what I felt the Lord had given me and asked if they felt I should I tell the man. The pastor right away said that he couldn't do it!

My sister and I began to discuss possible euphemisms I might use instead of horny. As we talked, I noticed that the man's wife got up from their table, perhaps to use the restroom? I felt I had to do it, so I rose from my chair, walked over, and sat next to Mr. Horny.

I had earlier introduced myself as an evangelist. As I gave him my newsletter and the gospel tract that I wrote, I informed him that sometimes the Lord gives me words for people, and I felt He had given me a word for him. I quietly said it was "horny." Then I asked, "Did I miss it?" He said, "You hit the nail right on the head!"

I asked him if I could pray for him, and he said I could. So, I laid hands on him and quietly prayed that the Lord would deliver him from impurity. Before his wife returned, I went back to my table.

A little later, he and his wife walked by our table as they were leaving the restaurant. He shook my hand and handed me the self-addressed return envelope included in my newsletter. When I got back to our rental car, I opened the envelope and inside was a fifty-dollar bill! I knew what the Lord was saying to me:

> **"If you are obedient and bold to share words that I give you for others, you will not only move them toward Me, but I will also provide all your needs financially to continue your prophetic ministry!"**

I was more motivated than ever to be used by the Lord to give people words. Despite the above stories of words I have given, remember, I am NOT a prophet. You don't have to be a prophet or have the "gift of prophecy" resting on your shoulders to prophesy!

"The testimony of Jesus is the spirit of prophecy."

Anyone who lifts the name of Jesus as a testimony of His grace and power is prophesying in a very real sense! Think about it: Which is the most significant prophetic insight?

A mighty Old-Testament prophet prophesying: "If you pray and obey, God is going to bless you financially and in every other way." Or today's Christian testifying: "Jesus is the only way to avoid an eternity in hell?"

That is an absolute no-brainer! Warning people to prepare for eternity is, in this evangelist's opinion, the most urgent word any human can utter! So, be a prophet to the people on your job, your school, and in your neighborhood through your witness for Christ! Tell the devil today:

My Testimony is a Prophecy!

Prophesy people out of hell! Yet, we know that the Lord is still very concerned about His Church's happiness and welfare on this side of eternity.

To any pastor or other church leader who happens to be reading this today, Paul has an urgent word for you:

"Let the prophets speak" (1 Cor. 14:29 KJV).

Make it easy for the prophetic gifts to operate in your church. "Prophets speak," so you'll need to step aside and let someone else in the pulpit at times (scary as that may be for you!).

The operation of all spiritual gifts is through imperfect vessels:

> **"We have this treasure in earthen vessels,**
> **that the excellency of the power might be of**
> **God and not of us"** (2 Corinthians 4:7 KJV).

Someone prophesying may have little wisdom but much motivation. Leaders can "judge" and keep "prophets" from going off the deep end. Those who prophesy sometimes even say foolish things! God knew this would happen when He made this gift available to His children.

> **"But God chose the foolish things of the world**
> **to shame the wise; God chose the weak things**
> **of the world to shame the strong"** (1 Cor. 1:27).

Are you one of those "foolish" or "weak" things? You aren't alone, and good news: God can use you! BUT you must always exercise self-control in the manifestation of prophetic gifts:

> **"The spirits of the prophets are subject to the**
> **prophet"** (1 Cor. 14:32).

The Spirit of God does not "force" a prophet (or anyone else for that matter) to say (or do) anything. Those prophesying are expected to exercise the fruit of the Spirit, self-control, when it comes to speaking words. ("The Spirit made me do it!" is not scripturally justifiable! No more than "The devil made me do it!")

Learn not just what to speak, but when to speak! Jesus once told His disciples:

> **"I still have many things to say to you, but you cannot bear them now"** (John 16:12).

It is not always wise to speak to people, even if what you are saying is the truth, especially if they couldn't "bear" it now (because they are already so hurt, still too immature, or not ready spiritually to receive it). Paul told the Corinthian church:

> **"And I, brethren, could not speak to you as to spiritual people but as to carnal, as to babes in Christ. I fed you with milk and not with solid food; for until now you were not able to receive it, and even now you are still not able; for you are still carnal"** (1 Cor. 3:1-3).

Paul didn't tell the church everything he would like to have told them! Prophetic people often want to "speak their mind," but this should only be done when it is in tune with 1 Corinthians 2:16, which reminds us:

> **"We have the mind of Christ."**

Peter was an Apostle, yet he once spoke with the "mind of the devil" (Matthew 16:22, 23). There is also a "fleshly mind" (Col. 2:18). If you desire to prophesy, pray for discernment to know the difference. (Pastor, you can and must help your people to do this!)

Furthermore, just because someone prophesying "thinks it" doesn't mean he must "speak it!"

> **"Let every man be quick to hear; slow to speak"** (James 1:19).

Paul prayed a prayer which showed that the best way for those who prophesy to speak words to others is by making sure they are always:

"speaking the truth in love" (Eph. 4:15).

"Speaking" words (no matter how fraught with truth) must always be undergirded by and given in a spirit of "love." Those who prophesy must never forget this!

1 Cor. 14:12 KJV says the Corinthian church was. . .

"zealous of spiritual gifts"

. . .which included prophecy. Still, Paul warned them to make sure they had the right motive in the manifestation of that gift:

"seek that ye may excel to the edifying (building up) **of the church."**

Prophetic words should edify and:

BUILD UP; (NOT) **BLOW UP!**

My sister, Elaine, believed she was called by God to be a prophet. She discovered that it would take decades of training and grooming before being "unleashed" on His Church. Several years back she traveled with me for nearly two years all over America, prophesying, training, and imparting her prophetic gift to the churches. She read many books, prayed many prayers, and listened and learned from many other prophets before her ministry was matured enough to "go with the gift."

Patiently study and learn more about prophesying so that when God finally "unleashes" you on His Body, in this last big league world series move of God, you will be seasoned, mature, and "safe" to minister. This need for maturity is especially true of those who prophesy because that gift is so volatile, easily misunderstood, or even hurtful if not given with love and wisdom.

"Speaking words" inspired by God, motivated by love, and spoken with wisdom is a foundational gift on which the church operates and grows. It's:

The Purpose of prophesying!

(If you are motivated to study this subject more thoroughly, you might do well to order one or more of the following books. They are all available at Amazon.com)

The Discerner: Hearing, Confirming, and Acting On Prophetic Revelation, James W. Goll, Whitaker House, 2017.

Releasing the Spirit of Prophecy: The Supernatural Power of Testimony, Bill Johnson, Destiny Image Publishers, 2014.

Prophets and Personal Prophecy, Dr. Bill Hamon, Destiny Image Publishers, 1987.

23

The Day of His Power

"Your people shall be volunteers in the day of Your power" (Psalm 110:3).

It was 1976. I was pastoring a church in Lakeview, Oregon. I had believed all my Christian life in the pre-tribulation rapture theory, but I noticed how leaders in the body of Christ were writing or speaking about the church being here for at least part of the Great Tribulation. I was confused and troubled over it.

I decided I would read through the book of Revelation, all the way through, with an open and teachable spirit. It was that year that I believe the Lord revealed two things to me, things that would set the course for the rest of my life. I saw:

1. The church will go through at least part of the Great Tribulation. I can't tell you how depressed I was for the next few weeks! I was expecting to escape all the terrible events you read about in John's writing. Now, I too must be one of the reluctant participants. I was not ready to suffer. I was not prepared for persecution. Over the next four-plus decades I studied the subject of Christ's coming and began to prepare

myself and others for some difficult days ahead: physically, emotionally, financially, and spiritually. (Email us at warford7@ hotmail.com, request it, and we will send you the complete study on why I believe in pre-wrath rapture)

2. God had called me especially for the last day reaping of lost souls on this planet. The healing mantle for which I had fasted and prayed and so often earnestly sought since I was a teenager would fall on my shoulders during that time. It was the power of God that would produce the fruit and prepare a people for His coming. I even "knew" that the primary purpose of my life was for that hour and would be fulfilled in this brief span of time.

As I aged through the years, I developed greater maturity (and less selfishness!) and an understanding that I was also to train, impart, and release others to do the same (thus this book in your hands!). I learned many things from John the Baptist.

John the Baptist

John the Baptist's ministry lasted only a short six to eighteen months (scholars estimate). John's ministry prepared the people for the first coming of Christ:

> **"He will also be filled with the Holy Spirit, even from his mother's womb. And he will turn many of the children of Israel to the Lord their God. He will also go before Him in the spirit and power of Elijah, 'to turn the hearts of the fathers to the children,' and the disobedient to the wisdom of the just, to make ready a people prepared for the Lord"** (Luke 1:15-17).

Notice several important truths we glean from these verses. John the Baptist:

"(was) **filled with the Holy Spirit.**"

(We didn't have space in this book to deal with the subject of how to be filled with the Holy Spirit. It has been written about many times before. For a full study of the subject, go to: Amazon.com and type "Baptism in the Holy Spirit." If you desire to be used of God, seek to "be filled with the Spirit.")

"**He will turn many. . .to the Lord.**"

(The biggest and most important final task on earth!)

"**He will go. . .in the spirit and power of Elijah.**"

(Elijah prophesied, healed the sick, and even raised the dead. John had that power too though he didn't work miracles. Miracles was a mantle Christ would wear and then return to earth to pass on to His church! It is available to us now and in an even greater measure in coming days!)

"**He will turn. . .the disobedient to the wisdom of the just.**"

(What is "the wisdom of the just?")

The wisdom of the just is:

1. The wisdom to heal the sick (refer to Chapter 8):

2. The wisdom to cast out demons (refer to Chapters 17-20):

> "**One who is wise can go up against the city of the mighty and pull down the stronghold in which they trust**" (Proverbs 21:22 NIV).

3. The wisdom to prophesy (refer to Chapters 21, 22):

"The wise in heart will receive commands"
(Proverbs 10:8).

4. The wisdom to win souls and get the church prepared for His coming (order my soul-winner's book: *EVANGELIST: MY LIFE STORY; MY LIFE JOURNEY* at Amazon.com):

"He who wins souls is wise" (Proverbs 11:30).

"to make ready a people prepared for the Lord."

Jesus is soon coming for the second time. I believe in preparation for that coming, God is going to sovereignly pour out His Spirit on His people again, giving them an anointing like John to prophesy to a world about to be burned with fire:

"Prepare to meet thy God" (Amos 4:12).

The Lord will need MANY workers to accomplish this, and He will likely be calling YOU:

"'Behold, I will send for MANY fishermen,' says the Lord, "and they shall fish them; and afterward I will send for many hunters, and they shall hunt them from every mountain and every hill, and out of the holes of the rocks" (Jeremiah 16:16).

The Church Versus the Devil

Jesus gave warnings about the last days:

>"False Messiahs and false prophets will
>appear. They will work spectacular,
>miraculous signs and do wonderful things to
>deceive, if possible, even those whom God
>has chosen" (Matthew 24:24 GW).

In Israel's last days in Egypt (after over 400 years of bondage!), there was a great confrontation between the power of God and Satan's power. This confrontation, I believe, is a prophetic picture of what is soon to come:

>"And Aaron cast down his rod before Pharaoh
>and before his servants, and it became a
>serpent. But Pharaoh also called the wise
>men and the sorcerers; so the magicians of
>Egypt, they also did in like manner with their
>enchantments. For every man threw down his
>rod, and they became serpents. But Aaron's
>rod swallowed up their rods" (Exodus 7:11-12).

God's superior power prevailed in that battle!

>"when Aaron stretched out his hand with the
>staff and struck the dust of the ground, gnats
>came on people and animals. All the dust
>throughout the land of Egypt became gnats.
>But when the magicians tried to produce
>gnats by their secret arts, they could not"
>(Exodus 8:17, 18).

The power of the devil's false prophets is nothing compared to the dunamis power of God's prophets! In the final countdown before our escape from this planet, we are going to give Hell a display of God's glory like it has feared for millennia:

> **"His intent was that now, through the church, the manifold wisdom of God should be made known to the rulers and authorities in the heavenly realms"** (Ephesians 3:10 NIV).

"Through the church" God's wisdom to outwit the enemy will be "made known" to all of Satan's kingdom. However, that will not happen without a battle of the ages. And that is why, I believe, the Lord revealed to me that we will still be here for part of the Great Tribulation. We must be prepared.

The Coming Persecution

The coming persecution will help fan the flames of coming Holy Spirit power. Philip was just a deacon in the church, waiting on tables, but persecution brought an end to that phase of his ministry and launced an entirely new one (refer to Chapter 6):

> **"a great persecution broke out against the church in Jerusalem, and all except the apostles were scattered throughout Judea and Samaria. . .Those who had been scattered preached the word wherever they went. Philip went down to a city in Samaria"** (Acts 8:1-5).

You already read in Chapter 6 about the miracles of healing and deliverance and city-wide revival that broke out through Philip's ministry. That would not have happened had it not been for "a great persecution." Well, great persecution is coming to America (you surely see the signs already here!).

I find great inspiration from the two witnesses in Revelation 11:3-6 (NIV):

> **"And I will appoint my two witnesses, and they will prophesy for 1,260 days, clothed in sackcloth. If anyone tries to harm them, fire comes from their mouths and devours their enemies. . .They have power to shut up the heavens so that it will not rain during the time they are prophesying; and they have power to turn the waters into blood and to strike the earth with every kind of plague as often as they want:"**

Take special notice of a specified time their ministry will last: "for 1260 days." That is their destined length of ministry. No demon from Hell will be able to touch them all that time.

These two men will be "witnesses." They also "will prophesy." And they will perform great miracles, similar to signs that were performed in Egypt. Their conflict with the devil will last about 3½ years and then:

> **"When they finish their testimony, the beast that ascends out of the bottomless pit will make war against them, overcome them, and kill them"** (Revelation 11:7).

Yes, persecution will put an end to the two witnesses destined ministry, but it won't happen until:

> **"they finish their testimony."**

Hallelujah! Think of it! You can "finish" your business for the kingdom. If you will walk with the Lord and obey his directions in this coming conflict:

> **You are immortal until you fulfill your destiny!**

Your last day's destiny is to be a witness, heal the sick, cast out devils, and prophesy! Your persecutors won't be able to touch you (you'll pass right through them just like Jesus did or walk out of a locked prison as Peter did!) until your 1260 (365, 927, 1272?) days are completed. You WILL "finish your testimony." This "day of power" will be exciting for sure:

God's Volunteers

> **"Your people shall be volunteers in the day of Your power; In the beauties of holiness, from the womb of the morning, You have the dew of Your youth"** (Psalm 110:3).

The last day army is a "volunteer" army. God won't make you go out as a witness during persecution or hardships. You can hide in your closet. Or you can go out by faith and experience His glorious power outpoured!

Be prepared, volunteer! There are three supernatural works the Lord will make available to you in this "day of His power":

1. "the beauties of holiness"

It doesn't say "in the beauties of love" or "in the beauty of grace." In the final battle of good versus evil, HOLINESS will be the most important attribute of His army. 2 Timothy 2:1-22 gives us one of the best descriptions of the requirement for God's "volunteers":

> **"You therefore must endure hardship as a good soldier of Jesus Christ...Therefore I endure all things for the sake of the elect, that they also may obtain the salvation which is in Christ. . .Be diligent to present yourself approved to God, a worker who does not need to be ashamed, rightly dividing the word of truth. . ."Let everyone who names the name of Christ depart from iniquity." Therefore if anyone cleanses himself. . .he will be a vessel for honor, sanctified and useful for the Master, prepared for every good work. Flee also youthful lusts; but pursue righteousness"**

Note especially the phrases: "depart from iniquity, cleanses himself, sanctified (holy), prepared, flee. . .lusts." Not every Christian is ready spiritually for what is ahead for us. They are living unholy lives. If you are wise, you will repent now, learn to live a holy life, and then (and only then), when you are needed the most, you will be "useful for the master."

2. "from the womb of the morning"

A "womb" is the place where babies grow. I see in this a beautiful picture of God's army rising early to find a place of devotion with the Lord (night owl, I suppose your pattern of waiting until everyone is in bed to have your devotional time is applicable too). Our prayer and Bible study will be the absolute foundation for us all during the last days:

"With my soul I have desired You in the night, Yes, by my spirit within me I will seek You early; For when Your judgments are in the earth, The inhabitants of the world will learn righteousness" (Isaiah 26:9).

Let that be your confession and habit starting NOW: "I will seek you early." When the Kingdom of God is about to be established on this planet, we must before all else:

"Seek first the kingdom of God and His righteousness" (Matthew 6:33).

Our calling is to seek the Kingdom's power and glory manifested through our lives. But not just that: to also be walking victoriously in "His righteousness."

3. "You have the dew of Your youth."

This phrase is exceptionally important to me now that I am in my seventies. For a few years, I have felt like I fight tiredness more than I do the devil! If the vision God has given me to be an instrument of power in the last days is fulfilled, I will need an infusion of new physical strength. Some of you older folks may feel as I do. Well, I suggest you do what I did! I wrote a big note for my desk that says:

"I have the dew of my youth!"

I am claiming that even today! There are other promises of renewed strength to face the coming battle (Isaiah 40:29-31; Psalm 18:32; 27:1; 29:11; 31:24; 119:28; 138:3). I especially like this one:

"You have armed me with strength for the battle" (Psalm 18:39).

I claim promises for strength, but that is not all I do. I am counting on being here and ministering even into my eighties! I must have the strength to carry the dunamis into the battle! I am so serious about this that I made major changes in my life as I aged. I run two miles and lift weights and have done so since my fifties. I eat a pretty nutritious diet. I often drink blender smoothies made with water, raw vegetables (usually four ounces of fresh red cabbage and four ounces of frozen broccoli), raw fruits, nuts, and seeds (I had another one this morning before I caught my flight to Denver).

Doesn't that taste awful, you might ask? What does taste have to do with being a strong soldier!? I have a more critical "taste" to be concerned about:

"Taste and see that the Lord is good"
(Psalm 34:8).

This verse is an invitation to those who don't know the Lord. That's what we want to concentrate on doing in the last days: passing out invitations to be seated at the table of the marriage supper of the Lamb!

This would be a good time to remind you that fasting (sacrificing "taste") was an essential facet of the Healing Revival (refer to Chapter 2). Fasting will come to the forefront again in the next healing revival. Start practicing now.

I recommend no-pleasant bread fasts (see Daniel 10:2, 3). Anybody can do this, at any time, even when they are working a physically challenging job. You simply sacrifice tasty food, meat, and drink (or whatever you decide to do) as much as practical (Those with sugar diabetes can even use this type of fasting).

Anything you sacrifice to seek the Lord and show your devotion to Him is a form of fasting. For example, I have fasted newspapers till noon. I fasted football one season until the Rose Bowl. My wife and I fasted television for a month. I fasted sugar for forty days. Also, consider music, iPhones, or reading fiction books as something you are willing to set aside temporarily. Do your best to spend more time in prayer and the Word during such fasts. Let the Lord lead you and be obedient to His call to any special times of fasting and prayer.

Be Patient!

Consider that I started fasting and praying for a ministry of supernatural miracles when I was but 21 years of age. I certainly didn't imagine for a moment that I would still be waiting today for that fire to fall on me. I have seen many miracles of healing and deliverance in my lifetime, for which I am truly grateful. But I am not satisfied yet; I know there is more!

I was speaking in Oregon a couple of decades ago. I was stepping out in faith, giving words of knowledge, seeking to get people healed. The results were very minimal. When I got back to the house where I was staying for the revival, I felt discouraged and disappointed. Seeking comfort, I asked the Lord for a word about why I didn't see more results that night. I turned to Daniel 8:17:

> **"'Understand, son of man, that the vision refers to the time of the end.'"**

This was a clear confirmation, to me, of the same revelation I had received decades earlier: my supernatural ministry to which God called me is primarily for the last days ("the time of the end").

Recently I was lamenting again the disappointment I was experiencing in my ministry, especially after reading again some of the testimonies to put in this book. I asked the Lord: "Why am I not seeing the miracles of healing I used to see?" I turned in my Bible to Revelation 14:7:

> **"Fear God, and give glory to Him; for the hour of his judgment has come."**

That was at least the third witness that the glory of God will be most visible in my life during the last few months or years of time ("the hour of His judgment"). Patience is one of the most needed fruits of the Spirit in last day saints:

> **'Staying with it - that's what is required. Stay with it to the end"** (Luke 21:19 MSG).

The persecution we may soon have to endure calls for patience:

> **"If anyone is to go into captivity, into captivity they will go. If anyone is to be killed with the sword, with the sword they will be killed." This calls for patient endurance and faithfulness on the part of God's people"** (Revelation 13:10 MSG).

Don't fret about this:

> **"we will receive mercy and find grace to help us just when we need it"** (Hebrews 4:16; GNT).

Stop worrying about persecution! Rather, look at the glory we will enjoy during it all. Remember, the Lord saves the "best wine for last" (John 2).

Signs and Wonders

At the end of Paul's days, he was on an island. A snake fastened to his hand, but he just shook it off (Acts 28:5). The islanders watched in anticipation for him to die, but he didn't. This reminds us of the authority we have in Mark 16:18 to "take up serpents." We are going to be doing that to a lot of serpents (demons) in the coming deliverance revival! Then something even more dramatic took place on the island:

> **"And it happened that the father of Publius
> lay sick of a fever and dysentery. Paul went
> in to him and prayed, and he laid his hands
> on him and healed him. So when this was
> done, the rest of those on the island who had
> diseases also came and were healed"**
> (Acts 28:8,9).

Miracles of healing brought revival to a whole island!

Miracles of healing brought revival to a whole town in Samaria (see Acts 8)!

Miracles in your life and your church will bring revival to YOUR city!

Recently something happened that encouraged me that the new anointing for signs and wonders is about to, at last, fall on me and YOU! (I believe the Lord specifically had it happen so I could put the story in this book as a witness to what I am communicating in this chapter!) It happened while I was ministering at the Big Bear, California Foursquare Church. Let her tell her own story:

"My name is Doris Meneses. About 3 years ago, Dea laid hands on me and the Lord healed me of vertigo. I had suffered with it, 24/7, for about ten years. I fell all the time. To get to my car from the store where I worked, I at times had to take a grocery cart to push myself to my car because I was so busy. I was a cake decorator and had to lean against a wall to decorate. I would see doctors. They'd give me medication, but nothing ever worked. After my healing, it was amazing! I was literally running back and forth with my eyes closed. At times the enemy will attack and I will feel it but I get verbal and say "Get away! I have been healed of this!" So, I have to take a stand against that. I had a heart attack about a year ago, so I am being treated for that and I am on medication. When I came in today, I know the enemy was trying to keep me away from coming, because I started having heart palpitations, pain in my chest, and shortness of breath. But I said, "I am not going to receive this today." So, I came into the church, and I am just sitting here, and the heart palpitations and the shortness of breath is going strong on me. I thought to myself, "I may have to leave and go home because it was coming on so strong." Then, before the service had even started, Dea came over and patted me on the back and while he was doing that, I felt the power of God. Immediately, my heart stopped palpitating and the shortness of breath ceased. Literally, I can take a deep breath! The sharp pain had gone away, throughout the service, and it is gone right now! I can take a deep breath! Thank You Father!"

All I did was greet Doris and pat her on the back! Yet, the dunamis was transmitted through a believer's hand. Of course, it was His Hand on mine:

> **"His brightness was like the light; He had rays flashing from His hand, And there His power was hidden"** (Habakkuk 3:4).

I wasn't fasting that day. I had been in one of the busiest seasons of my life (writing this book among other things) yet a miracle happened just by a nonchalant touch! It's a harbinger of power encounters coming soon. To reap the final harvest, we need God's Hand upon us. We now need to again pray as the early disciples prayed:

> **"Grant to Your servants that with all boldness they may speak Your word, by stretching out Your HAND to heal, and that signs and wonders may be done"** (Acts 4:29, 30).

God answered their prayer and we read of miracle after miracle throughout the rest of the book of Acts:

> **"And with GREAT POWER the apostles gave WITNESS to the resurrection of the Lord Jesus. And great GRACE was upon them all"** (Acts 4:33).

Doris' testimony is NOT a tribute to my power, it is a tribute to the grace of God! And this GRACE will soon be poured out in an ever-increasing measure.

A Sneak Preview

Nearly two decades ago, the Lord gave me what I know is a "SNEAK PREVIEW" of things to come. I was preaching a revival at the Assembly of God Church in Palm Springs, California. One evening, I preached on spiritual warfare. I called folks forward for prayer. There was maybe a line of a dozen or so adults.

As I slowly moved down the line, laying hands on each of them, demons began to manifest. It seemed that everyone in the line was coughing, shaking, or jerking and/or everything that demons like to do when they are being commanded to come out! I had never seen that high a percentage of demonic manifestations at the altar.

During another service at the church, while preaching, I noticed three young people sitting together towards the back. They looked at me poker-faced, staring at me emotionless while I preached. I thought maybe they had smoked marijuana before the service! When I gave the altar call, of course, I was especially mindful of the need of these three to come forward and get right with God.

I kept glancing at them, looking for even one hand to rise. Sadly, nothing I said could get them to budge. So, I changed the order of the service and began praying for the sick.

A man with one leg shorter than the other came up for prayer. Seeing this as an opportunity to help people who might have never seen a miracle to at last see one, I had him come up to the platform and sat him on a chair. I purposely placed him and the chair sideways, so the congregants would have a good view of what might happen.

I lifted his feet horizontally, with his shoes still on. The palm of my hand was holding his legs up by his Achilles Tendons (I did this purposely, so no one would think I was "pulling" on his leg! You know the reputation healing evangelists have for being phonies!). I began explaining to the people what I was about to do, but before I had a chance to even pray, something dramatic happened. In sight of everyone, that shorter leg popped out to the same length as the other one!

People were excited and began rejoicing over the miracle they had just witnessed. I calmed everybody down and said:

> **"You have just witnessed the power of God in a demonstration. He is real! Don't you want Him in your life? If you do, come down to this altar right now."**

Two of those three young people came forward to receive Christ! My best gospel preaching hadn't moved them an inch. One visible miracle did!

One manifestation of the Holy Spirit's power "preaches" better than a 10,000 word sermon!

Don't you want miracles in your life to help you win the lost? That power is on its way!

Our Grand Finale

The best way to end this book would be not just more testimonies of men and women but the testimony of the scriptures. See what the Bible says about our grand finale! Visualize yourself fulfilling these promises:

"So shall they fear The name of the Lord from the west, And His glory from the rising of the sun; When the enemy comes in like a flood (that will happen during the last days. Deliverers will be desperately needed!), **The Spirit of the Lord will lift up a standard against him. The Redeemer will come to Zion, And to those who turn from transgression in Jacob"** (Isaiah 59:19-21).

"For behold, the day is coming, Burning like an oven, And all the proud, yes, all who do wickedly will be stubble. And the day which is coming shall burn them up (evidence: this is during terrible times, times of judgment!) **says the Lord of hosts. . .But to YOU who fear My name The Sun of Righteousness shall arise With HEALING** (you'll heal the sick by His power) **in His wings"** (Mal. 4:1, 2).

'**And it shall come to pass in the last days** (yes, this is a last day special coming event!), **says God, That I will pour out of My Spirit on all flesh; Your sons and your daughters** (this will be a special visitation on our children and teenagers. Oh, how desperately they need it because of how the media has defiled them!) **shall PROPHESY. Your young men shall see visions, Your old men** (hallelujah! that's me!) **shall dream dreams. And on My menservants** (are you His servant?) **and on My maidservants I will pour out My Spirit in those days; And they shall prophesy. I will show wonders in heaven above and signs in the earth beneath** (then, check out the evidence: this outpouring happens shortly before calamities like. . .): **Blood and fire and vapor of smoke."** (Acts 2:17-21).

"Repent therefore and be converted, that your sins may be blotted out so that times of refreshing (repentance must be preached for revival to happen!) **may come from the presence of the Lord, and that He may send Jesus Christ, who was preached to you before, whom heaven must receive UNTIL** (Jesus will NOT come before the greatest revival!) **the TIMES of restoration of all things, which God has spoken by the mouth of all His holy prophets** (everything God promised would happen will happen!) **since the world began"** (Acts 3:19-21).

"Most assuredly, I say to you, he who believes in Me, the works that I do he will do also; and greater works than these he will do, because I go to My Father" (John 14:12).

Jesus healed the sick, cast out demons, prophesied and even raised the dead. He promised we would do "greater works" than even He performed. But this will not happen to those who are sitting and doing nothing. We must pray and believe for it:

"And whatever you ask in My name, that I will do, that the Father may be glorified in the Son. If you ask ANYTHING in My name, I will do it." (John 4:13, 14).

Notice that bold ANYTHING! As I finish this last chapter of this book today, I look forward to tomorrow. It just happens to be Pentecost Sunday. That is the once-a-year Sunday when the church celebrates the day of the first outpouring of Holy Spirit power on His church. I will be asking "anything" as Jesus promised.

My anything is that signs and wonders will be manifested in the church in Laramie, Wyoming where I am speaking.

What is your "anything?" I hope it will be prayers for the dunamis to heal the sick, cast out devils, and prophesy. There will be a price to pay (and to pray!) for the power; there always has been and always will. Prayer, fasting, bearing your cross, obedience, facing persecution is your duty. Nevertheless, God will give you grace. However, it will not come without a fight:

> **"From the time John preached his message until this very day the Kingdom of heaven has suffered violent attacks, and violent men try to seize it"** (Matthew 11:12).

We must be violent: passionate, energetic, boldly fighting. We must be violent against sin, violent against disease, violent against demonic powers, violently prophesying. We must "try to seize it (the Kingdom's power and promise)" against all "violent attacks" from the enemy!

Don't watch the Kingdom happen to and in others! Seize it for yourself!

> **"the Good News about the Kingdom of God is being told, and everyone forces their way in"** (Luke 16:16 GNT).

Sinners will not be saved and will miss the rapture unless they repent and "force their way in" to the church! To help them do that we must preach the Good News to them, but NOT with just words:

"For our gospel did not come to you in word only, but also in power, and in the Holy Spirit" (1 Thessalonians 1:5).

Force your "way in" to the place of power that is so abundantly provided by the Holy Spirit: power to heal the sick, cast out demons, and prophesy. I trust that this book has succeeded in helping convince you of this glorious truth:

MIRACLES ARE YOUR DESTINY

Epilogue

""She has fallen! Great Babylon has fallen! She is now HAUNTED by demons and unclean spirits . . . For all the nations have drunk her... strong wine of her immoral lust. The kings of the earth practiced sexual immorality with her, and the merchants of the world grew rich from her unrestrained lust"
(Revelation 18:2, 3 GNT).

Many believe that "Babylon the great" is the United States, or possibly New York City. America is indeed much like ancient Babylon (which means "confusion"). Many of our nation's leaders, schools and colleges, the media, and Hollywood are absurdly confused about our human sexuality. This confusion is nothing less than the stratagem of hell. Much of the USA has become "HAUNTED" by demons, who reveal their character through sexually deviant behavior, "her immoral lust."

I thought chapter 23 was the closing chapter of this book. Then, just this morning, I received a phone call from a lady who gave me the following (we'll keep anonymous) testimony. I know this was the Holy Spirit's doing. It vividly shows what we will be up against in the last days, Babylon's "unrestrained lust."

"One of my brother's friends and my uncle molested me (not rape but touches that I discerned were wrong). My whole life, from an early age, maybe eight years old,

I was hypersexual, obsessed with thinking about sex and masturbating. While playing with Barbie Dolls with my friends, I would try to get them to show me their private parts. With that came feelings of anger, being misunderstood, and feeling alone, because none of my other friends acted that way.

"I would have night terrors and panic attacks. I often heard the voice of the devil in my mind. To the tune of "Mary had a Little Lamb," Satan would sing to me, "Jesus is going to rape you! Jesus is going to rape you!" I would have dreams about demons raping me. Afterward, I would see the face of my father (who hadn't done that) or other men and boys I knew. Upon waking up, I felt such shame!

"At twelve years old, I was saved at a Carmen concert. I started reading the Bible, but I didn't lay down my sin. I always repented of my sin and asked God to forgive me but went right back to it repeatedly. As an adult, the hypersexuality continued. I cheated on everybody I had ever been with. My 3rd husband asked me, "Have you ever thought about swinging (with another man)?" I didn't like the idea but did it anyway. My husband wanted me to stay a sinner. He was into pornography. I was into it too. With me, it was like an addict trying to get a fix. I was angry at the drop of a hat.

"In 2020, I was in my thirties. When Dea came to our church and spoke, he afterward stood at the altar to pray for people. When he asked me what my problem was, I didn't say, "hypersexuality and sexual addiction." I said, "extreme anger." Then he prayed over me. Instantly, my whole body felt tingly, with goosebumps. My knees were knocking uncontrollably. When I went home, I prayed, "Let me be healed."

"That was the beginning of my true sanctification. I laid down all sin. I started paying close attention to the "triggers". No more adultery or masturbation, rather laying down face down on the floor, laying it at the cross. It has been beautiful! It was like that lifelong addiction had been cast out. I thought, "Victory! I am a new woman and healed."

"But then the Lord spoke to me and said, "We're not done yet." I knew I still had to deal with anger, anxiety and night terrors, and the demons raping me. I had had nightmares and night terrors about twice a night all my life! After my deliverance, I had just two more of these dreams. I woke up crying after the first one and said, "No, I will not go back to that!" Then I learned about the importance of putting on the armor of God and rebuking the enemy. I was then able to overcome those demonic attacks.

"Right after I got delivered, I left my husband. I spent ten days over 1000 miles away from him. I love him, but I knew I couldn't be unequally yoked to him the way he was. I bought a house and was painting it and cleaning it up. I even bought furniture because I felt that I had left him. On the 10th day, my mother said to me, "You know you can forgive him." I hadn't even thought about forgiving him. I knew I had been forgiven, but now I determined that I could forgive him also.

"The next day, I had a strong pull to come back to my husband, so I left and returned to him. When I got home, I announced, "I will never let any man drag me to hell again! Don't ever talk to me about the sin or ask me to do it!" He said, "Ok." He was an agnostic, but he stopped looking at pornography because he didn't want to lose me. One night, he was sitting at a bar, talking to a stranger. He told the man who was smoking and chewing like he was, "I am trying to stop smoking, chewing, and drinking. I also want to live for Jesus." With that, he felt an amazing feeling come over him. It was like a pain (tingle) throughout the whole body. He started weeping uncontrollably. He even felt Jesus standing next to him.

"At 11 PM, he ran home in the rain, pounded up the stairs, and threw himself over my legs, weeping. He then told me,

'I felt Jesus standing next to me, and I want to live for Him.'

"I led him in the sinner's prayer! He is a new man. He started taking the initiative and prays before meals. He goes to church every Sunday and to Bible studies. It was the most extreme change I have ever seen. We both got baptized in water, along with one of our children. We are both happy."

Her testimony is an example of the truth that no matter how Satan attacks the church with his Revelation 12:12 "great wrath," the Lord will still use us to bring deliverance to His people.

Not only that, the manifestation of the dunamis He has given us all will win the lost! A world of sinners caught up in the spirit of the age (which is hypersexuality) will come to the Lord because of the "sign-gifts" of healings, deliverances, and prophetic words we bring. This will all be in fulfillment of Isaiah 60:1-3:

> **Arise, shine; For your light has come! And the glory of the Lord is risen upon you. For behold, the darkness shall cover the earth And deep darkness the people** (evidence: this is during times of great darkness; don't we see this in America now, especially concerning sexuality?) **but the Lord will arise over you, And His glory** (the power, the dunamis!) **will be SEEN upon you. The Gentiles shall come to your light, And kings. . .**
>
> (DRUM ROLL!)
>
> **. . . to the brightness of your rising."**

"Deep darkness" will soon "cover the earth." That's the bad news. The good news is darkness only makes the light shine even brighter! The Church of Jesus Christ is about to shine more brightly than it has ever shined! It is then that a desperately bound world will "come to your light."

Shine your brightness to a world covered in darkness!

Rise up, man or woman of God!

At the risk of being too repetitious, may I dare challenge just one more time to. . .

Heal the sick!

Cast out demons!

Prophesy!

**"And these signs will follow those who believe:
In My name they will cast out demons; they
will speak with new tongues; they will take up
serpents; and if they drink anything deadly, it
will by no means hurt them; they will lay hands
on the sick, and they will recover. . .And they
went out and preached everywhere, the Lord
working with them and confirming the word
through the accompanying signs. Amen."**
(Mark 16:17-20).

Evangelist Dea Warford

E-mail: warford7@hotmail.com
deawarford@gmail.com

To receive Dea's daily E-mail teachings in your inbox, free of
charge, sign up today by going to our website:

www.deawarford.org

(If you haven't already, be sure to order Dea's fascinating autobiography,
which includes special helps for those who desire to win souls:
EVANGELIST MY LIFE STORY: MY LIFE JOURNEY)

You may order it, and also order more copies of this book in either
paperback or hardback, from our website, or at: Amazon.com

Made in the USA
Monee, IL
04 November 2021